LEEDS UNITED

IN THE 1980s AND 1990s

LEEDS UNITED

IN THE 1980s AND 1990s

From Wilderness Years to Wilko

DAVE TOMLINSON

AMBERLEY

First published 2023

Amberley Publishing
The Hill, Stroud
Gloucestershire, GL5 4EP

www.amberley-books.com

British Library Cataloguing in Publication Data.
A catalogue record for this book is available from the British Library.

ISBN 978 1 3981 1419 7 (paperback)
ISBN 978 1 3981 1420 3 (ebook)

1 2 3 4 5 6 7 8 9 10

Typeset in 10pt on 13.5pt Sabon.
Typesetting by SJmagic DESIGN SERVICES, India.
Printed in Great Britain.

Printed and bound in Great Britain by TJ Books Limited, Padstow, Cornwall

Contents

Prologue: The Squalor of Leeds   7

Chapter One: Wrong Man, Wrong Time   11

Chapter Two: Sniffer   17

Chapter Three: Good Riddance to Bad Rubbish   22

Chapter Four: Into the Wilderness   28

Chapter Five: Ringing the Changes   34

Chapter Six: A Tragic Season   39

Chapter Seven: The King Is Dead, Long Live the King   44

Chapter Eight: Edge of Glory   49

Chapter Nine: Why Would Maradona Want to Come *Here*?   58

Chapter Ten: Marching Altogether   63

Chapter Eleven: Wilko   69

Chapter Twelve: The Big Push   74

Chapter Thirteen: In the Limelight and Loving It   83

Chapter Fourteen: Rosettes and Roast Lamb   89

Chapter Fifteen: Au Revoir   98

Chapter Sixteen: Recovery   105

Chapter Seventeen: Rebuilding   110

Chapter Eighteen: Raging Bull   114

Chapter Nineteen: Caspian: The Root of All Evil   122

Chapter Twenty: Hasselbaink   128

Chapter Twenty-one: Goodbye, Gorgeous George   137

Chapter Twenty-two: A Naïve Young Manager   142

Chapter Twenty-three: A Meteoric Rise   146

Chapter Twenty-four: Reflections   157

Bibliography   160

The Squalor of Leeds

And did those feet in ancient times,
Walk upon England's mountains green:
And was the holy lamb of God,
On England's pleasant pastures seen?

And did the Countenance Divine,
Shine forth upon our clouded hills?
And was Jerusalem builded here,
Among these dark satanic mills?

'Jerusalem' by William Blake

8 September 1979

Kev had just missed his first Leeds United game in five years. The football played by Jimmy Adamson's side was so God-awful dull that Kev had almost given up on the club.

The 7-0 thrashing they suffered earlier in the week at Arsenal might have been the nadir, but Kev had been losing heart for months. Tony Currie's defection in the summer was the final straw.

Kev didn't have the money to travel to Nottingham that afternoon to see Leeds play Forest as well as going to Queens Hall, the music venue that had begun life as Swinegate Tram Depot and was staging the first Futurama Festival that evening. The thought of taking in Public Image Limited, Joy Division and fifteen other acts appealed more than watching the shapeless football played by Kevin Hird, Alan Curtis and Ray Hankin. The choice was a no contest; the football was futile, the music massive.

The 26,914 people who watched a dull-as-dishwater goalless draw at the City Ground would have understood.

Kev had a high old evening, seeing Ian Curtis and Johnny (Rotten) Lydon up-close and personal. He wandered home in the wee small hours dripping with sweat, having danced himself to death. 'What a f***ing night!'

He rushed out to buy the *New Musical Express* the following Thursday to read a review of the gig. He was struck by the headline – 'Set the controls for the squalor of Leeds.'

'Says it all,' thought Kev to himself.

Leeds was a grim and depressing place at the end of the 1970s; the football was one thing, the city another. Kev, like many other young locals, lost his job as the industrial heartland of the north lost its way, undermined by the 'let the market rip' policies of Margaret Thatcher's new government. The situation worsened in the months to come as a full-blown recession gripped the nation.

Adding to the desolate atmosphere was the spectre of serial killer Peter Sutcliffe, 'The Yorkshire Ripper', responsible for thirteen murders of women between 1975 and his arrest in 1981.

Music promoter John Keenan, the brains behind Futurama, told *Dazed* magazine that Sutcliffe 'held the city to ransom', creating a climate of fear. Leeds was a bit of a dump in those days, a dark and gloomy industrial city. The whole of Boar Lane was crumbling and the pavements were dug up. It was a pretty gloomy city. They didn't clean the buildings and there was a lot of pollution. All the buildings were blackened with exhaust fumes, and it just had a depressing feel to it. The Ripper had been on the loose for a few years and there was an atmosphere of 'What's he going to do next?' People were paranoid. They didn't want to go out, parents didn't want their daughters to go out on their own, or even with friends.

The backstreets and alleyways of Yorkshire were a place of anxiety and fear as the 1980s dawned, the public still coming to terms with the murder of twenty-year-old student Barbara Leach in Bradford four months earlier. She was thought to be the eleventh victim of the Ripper.

Still convinced by the fake tape recordings received from a man claiming to be the killer, West Yorkshire Police regularly visited pubs around Leeds asking if anyone recognised the thick Geordie tones.

Whenever they asked the question of a football fan, they would get the same response. 'That's Jimmy Adamson that is, lock him up.'

The joke was in questionable taste, but the manager of Leeds United was almost as unpopular in the city as the man who had spent the previous five years murdering women. Even sharing his Ashington birthplace with Jack

Charlton, one of the club's legendary heroes, offered Adamson no respite – his inept management of United had made him a marked man.

The world had come tumbling down for Adamson after a charmed life in his first year at the club. His first nineteen league games had been marred by just one defeat, providing the launching pad for a fifth-place finish and qualification for European competition for the first time since the days of Don Revie. What more could United fans have wanted?

But they were a fickle and cynical lot, unimpressed by the latest man to try and match the achievements of Revie, still a god for United followers. Revie's thirteen years at the helm of Leeds United had delivered unprecedented success and set a high bar for any replacement.

A listless defeat against Southampton in the semi-finals of the League Cup and the summer departures of fans' favourites Tony Currie and Frank Gray had dulled the sheen on Adamson's first year in charge. It was the departure of Currie, the talisman, that really did for him.

Currie had lorded it at Elland Road ever since his arrival in 1976, bringing elegance and flair to a grey and dismal arena. The fans loved the midfielder for his showmanship and memorable goals and he had carried Leeds through Adamson's first season. But he could stay no longer – the homesickness of wife Alison saw to that.

Currie's departure left a gaping void – without him Leeds United were a shapeless and hopeless mess, an ageing team with little going for them. They'd outperformed themselves in 1979 and now the rot had set in.

'Adamson Out' chants filled the evening air. There was a tepid welcome for Adamson's nondescript transfer targets, a bunch of journeymen. 'You don't know what you're doing,' the fans bellowed from the stands.

Leeds plunged to 19th with UEFA Cup hopes shattered by two defeats to the unknown Romanians Universitatea Craiova. Six unbeaten games steadied the ship, but the fans refused to warm to Adamson. The board gave him the dreaded vote of confidence in a vain attempt to quell the unrest.

It was only six years since Revie had led Leeds United to their second league title, but that was a lifetime for downcast fans, fewer in number now, driven away by the hooliganism that dogged the club. Sections of the ground were closed off after missiles were thrown at players and the mood was frequently ugly in an empty stadium.

Leeds United was a club going nowhere but down, their reputation in the gutter. This was not a club in crisis – no one cared enough anymore for this to be a crisis. A slow, lingering, chronic sickness had squeezed hope out of the place.

The stench of urine emanating from the neglected toilets in the Elland Road stadium was a stark symbol of a club that offered little but a depressing and dangerous place to waste away a bleak Saturday afternoon.

And as the club collapsed and fell into disrepair, so too did the entire city. No jobs, no fun, no future – the atmosphere was as dark as the music of the goth movement that sprang up in Yorkshire. Leeds and its surroundings had a desperate and depressing feel to it. Where once football had offered an escape, now it offered only hooliganism, racists outside the ground and piss-poor players.

The Slough of Despond into which Leeds United had so cluelessly meandered was deep and cloying. In LS11 apathy reigned supreme.

'The Squalor of Leeds' did indeed say it all.

CHAPTER ONE

Wrong Man, Wrong Time

It was well into the depths of the bitterly cold evening of New Year's Day 1980. Leeds United manager Jimmy Adamson gazed across the frozen playing surface inside the Elland Road stadium, the white clouds of his breath giving the place an eerie feel. He appeared to be searching for divine inspiration.

It was a miracle that Leeds and Derby County had been able to play earlier that evening, so hard and treacherous was the pitch. The undersoil heating had been on continuously for three days but doubts persisted throughout the evening whether the game could be played to a finish.

'Without the heating, we could not possibly have played,' Adamson told the press, adding that referee Kevin McNally was in two minds after inspecting the frost-covered ground at the break. 'He said he had difficulty keeping his feet and obviously it was worse for players moving at speed and challenging for the ball. It was hard down the middle but softer on the wings which took a slight stud. We tossed up for ends before going on to the field so that the players could put in the best studs for the conditions.'

United were fortunate to scrape a victory against their relegation-haunted opponents, the 78th-minute goal a controversial one.

The linesman had furiously flagged for a foul when Leeds winger Carl Harris impeded Derby's Steve Buckley but the referee waved play on and Harris' telling cross drew a handball from defender Steve Powell on the edge of the Rams' area. Kevin Hird arrowed the free kick past Derby's undisciplined wall to secure the points.

The game had been messy, with little good football to keep the supporters warm. The points lifted Leeds to a flattering ninth, but Adamson was under no illusion that any corner had been turned.

Once again missing winger Arthur Graham and diminutive midfielder Brian Flynn, there was little colour or shape to Adamson's uninspired and uninspiring team. Eddie Gray and Harris had brought the only flair to a

11

laboured display. There were green shoots, however, with the promising form of two local teenagers – towering goalkeeper John Lukic and burly striker Terry Connor.

Lukic's first-team debut came in October, ten weeks before his nineteenth birthday. Two penalty saves and a string of sound displays in his first ten appearances persuaded Don Revie favourite David Harvey that his time at Elland Road was up. He opted for a new start at Vancouver Whitecaps following a March testimonial while Lukic marked himself out as the best young keeper in the First Division.

Connor was even younger. His debut against West Brom in November came a week after his seventeenth birthday. His goal settled the game and another strike at Old Trafford a month later made him a firm favourite with fans who harboured an irrational hatred for Manchester United.

Both players were still raw – Lukic was guilty of lapses in concentration and had conceded some howlers, while Connor was still learning how to harness his pace and strength. However, Adamson was patently aware of the paucity of a squad to which his summer signings had added little and he gambled that boys could grow into men overnight.

The manager knew that a sterner test than Derby lay ahead, with Leeds facing European Cup holders Nottingham Forest in the FA Cup. Even at Elland Road, Brian Clough's Forest would be a tough nut to crack.

Any shreds of optimism that Adamson took into the game were scattered within sixty seconds of kick-off as Eddie Gray's brother Frank, on his first return to Leeds, cracked home a stunning free kick. Forest won the game at a canter, 4-1, Leeds' only score coming from a haphazard own goal by Larry Lloyd.

'Adamson Out, Adamson Out!' boomed down from the terraces, the home fans turning spitefully on the manager. Adamson hung his head in silent despair. The fans had been calling for his head for months but he would never get used to it.

A shock victory at Arsenal was an anomaly as Leeds managed a single victory from the ten games that followed.

Adamson could offer nothing but cliché-ridden homilies. 'Luck wasn't with us today ... we're struggling with injuries ... I continue to enjoy the full support of the players and the board.'

His words cut no ice with increasingly hostile supporters, and 'Adamson Out' banners dominated a cold stadium.

Everyone knew where Leeds' problems lay: in a season where midfielder Kevin Hird top scored with eight in the league, three of them penalties, United managed only forty-six goals in forty-two games. As part of a flawed plan to rebuild, Adamson jettisoned top scorer John Hawley to Sunderland at the start of the season for £200,000 and took Wayne Entwistle in part-exchange.

The newcomer was just not ready for a team like Leeds and departed on a free transfer to Blackpool barely a year later.

A knee injury in January ended the season for big-money signing Alan Curtis, while an out of form Ray Hankin asked not to be considered for home games after being barracked by fans. The news brought a furious reaction from Adamson, who promptly sold Hankin to Vancouver Whitecaps. Carl Harris was another option but whiled away his season in the reserves with the manager unconvinced of his worth.

Adamson desperately pursued a proven goalscorer but his attempts to sign Kevin Keegan and Peter Withe were stymied by a board that balked at both the fees and the salaries. The reticence was perhaps understandable given the announcement of a loss of £820,363, a new record for a Football League club.

Adamson settled instead for the mundane talents of Rangers' Derek Parlane, bringing the front man to Elland Road in a £160,000 deal in March. A debut goal and victory against Southampton suggested he might be the answer but hopes faded as goals and points dried up.

Defensively, the two Pauls, Hart and Madeley, formed a decent partnership, while Trevor Cherry's withdrawal into the back four allowed Kevin Hird to operate in midfield where his awkward energy was less risky. There, he was ranged alongside Gary Hamson, Eddie Gray and Brian Flynn when the Welsh midfielder recovered fitness in the spring.

The heart and the fire had gone from Leeds, with few discernible signs of leadership. Jimmy Armfield had spent four painstaking years remodelling Revie's team, carefully recruiting to reshape the playing strength. Armfield's steady progress had been replaced by the lack of coherence that characterised Adamson's plan. Indeed, there were few who could detect any clear design in his random trawl of players from the lower divisions.

Fuelling rumours that the manager had a drinking problem, Adamson was often mysteriously absent from Elland Road. Preparations during the week by assistant manager Dave Merrington were often at odds with Adamson's matchday intentions. It was as if the two men were in different worlds, a bizarre situation given that they had worked together for fifteen years at Burnley and Sunderland.

Such matters were regular topics of conversation among the disillusioned fan base, the more critical of whom put it down to some weird plot to destroy Leeds United, that Adamson had an insane desire to right the wrongs of Don Revie's reign. He and the hierarchy he had served at Burnley had always been bitter critics of Revie, belying his public comment on arrival that Revie was 'one of the most successful managers we've had in the British game'.

It was all nonsense, of course, the reality one of cock-up rather than conspiracy. Adamson was merely past his best and incapable of tackling the challenge that faced him, the wrong man at the wrong time – Leeds United Football Club was falling apart under his management.

And yet, from out of the blue Adamson's team plucked out an end-of-season victory against the despised Manchester United at Elland Road. It presented the fans with a dilemma: do we continue to call for Adamson's head or cheer a famous victory?

A slick move saw an unmarked Parlane stroke Leeds into the lead inside the first quarter of an hour but Lukic and a resolute defence had to withstand concerted Manchester pressure in the second half. Victory was secured fourteen minutes from the end when Hird added a penalty after a questionable handball decision against pantomime villain Gordon McQueen, fiercely barracked by the crowd for his 'traitorous' defection to Old Trafford in 1978.

A glorious afternoon had no lasting impact, the fans quickly returning to their campaign for change.

Adamson's weary excuses filled the matchday programme. 'The last nine months have been disappointing,' he bleated, 'particularly when you look back and think of the optimism we all felt when the season got under way.' He acknowledged that 'by Leeds United's high standards, it has been a poor season' and quickly laid the blame on injuries. 'I cannot remember when we last had a fully fit first-team squad available and before our last home match against Villa we had nine senior players sidelined through injury plus two others suspended.'

Adamson was as aware as anyone that his grip on the job was tenuous, that he would never be able to win the fans round, but he prayed for something around the corner and hoped he could bumble through long enough for things to improve.

For once, he blanked the dour effort and solidity he prized so much and gambled £400,000 and his job on the gifted Argentine midfielder Alex Sabella, who had been making considerable waves at Sheffield United. The Blades had been relegated to the Third Division in 1979 and failure to earn promotion at the first attempt made Sabella's departure from Bramall Lane an inevitability. Adamson was only too ready to offer him an escape route.

Adamson had not a clue how best to use Sabella, but gave him a free role in the opening game of the new season at home to Aston Villa. Alan Curtis played lone striker but a midfield containing Eddie Gray, Carl Harris, Arthur Graham and Brian Flynn couldn't cope with a Villa side which was to end the season as champions.

The afternoon began brightly with Byron Stevenson stroking home a second-minute penalty after Flynn was fouled. It looked like a new beginning for Adamson but Leeds let Villa off the hook. By the half-hour mark, the visitors had taken command and equalised through Tony Morley. Gary Shaw added a second as the game reached the hour mark and it was clear long before the end that this was not to be Adamson's day.

Sabella had a couple of decent moments but the game passed him by, the afternoon ushered to a close by the familiar chants of 'Adamson Out'.

The bookies had long since stopped taking bets on Adamson as the first manager to be sacked and it looked a racing certainty when Leeds lost 3-0 to Middlesbrough in the next game. His voice remained calm and reassuring in interviews, but sleepless nights were pinching at his features.

There was an unanticipated glimmer of hope when Terry Connor scored a winner at Norwich with six minutes remaining. Adamson continued to believe, to hope there was a light at the end of the tunnel, that somehow this would all come right and he could yet make a success of the job.

Adamson's elation that night was obvious, a clenched-fist celebration when Connor's effort found the Norwich net concrete evidence of the eternal optimism of a football man.

Sabella had conjured up the chance from nowhere with a slippery shimmy through the Norwich ranks and Adamson believed that the little gem could yet be the saviour of both him and Leeds.

Deep inside, though, a gnawing reality was still there, the knowledge that this team was not good enough, that the fight had gone.

Defeat at home to Leicester the following weekend said it all, despite an early flourish.

The East Midlanders were fresh from victory against Bob Paisley's Liverpool and determined to show it was no flash in the pan – they worked double time to keep a revitalised Leeds at bay in an intense first half. Sabella was on fire, setting up two opportunities for Paul Hart to test keeper Mark Wallington and the woodwork. Just before the interval, the Argentine went close himself, leaving Leicester defenders dizzy as he danced through to wrongfoot Wallington with a veering left-foot drive but it swerved over instead of into the goal.

Leeds continued to force Leicester back and opened the scoring three minutes after the resumption. Again, it was Sabella who made it, setting up Hart to fire low into the net.

More clenched-fist celebrations from Adamson greeted the goal, but Leeds had no time to settle on the lead, Leicester levelling within two minutes. A free kick dropped towards the Leeds penalty spot and an unmarked John O'Neill had time to chest down before steering the ball past Lukic.

With seconds remaining, the Leeds defence yawned again. Alan Young nodded on for Martin Henderson to net a dramatic winner from the edge of the area.

Adamson, shattered by the late burst, told the media, 'It is important that I don't panic … I have a pool of good players and this was a finely balanced game throughout. It could have gone either way.'

A three-goal hammering at Stoke the following Saturday confirmed that time was up. By the Monday evening, it was done, a mutual agreement in place to end Adamson's contract, a guaranteed pay-off in return for falling on his own sword.

'The players need a new lift, the club needs a new lift, the supporters need a new lift,' admitted Adamson as he fronted it out.

His torture over, Adamson returned to Burnley to be with his family. He would never work again in football.

'Hey rock and roll, Adamson's on the dole,' chorused an unsympathetic Elland Road.

CHAPTER TWO

Sniffer

When it came, the removal of Jimmy Adamson was so rapid that Manny Cussins and the board had no time to develop a plan B. To give them breathing space, they availed themselves of the safe pair of hands offered by Maurice Lindley.

Revie's former assistant had been relied on before – he held the period in the weeks before Jimmy Armfield replaced Brian Clough in 1974, and again in the periods between Armfield and Jock Stein in 1978 and Stein and Adamson later that same year. He harboured no ambition for a long-term appointment but was always ready in time of need.

Lindley coaxed a decent performance out of the team in his one game in charge, a goalless draw at home to Tottenham. He rang the changes, replacing Brian Greenhoff, Brian Flynn, Paul Madeley and Gary Hamson with Kevin Hird, Byron Stevenson, Jeff Chandler and young Neil Firm, and moved Paul Hart forward into midfield. The reshaping worked wonders, as Don Warters reported in the *Yorkshire Evening Post*. 'United showed tremendous spirit as they fought gamely against one of the country's most improved outfits. It must have been rewarding for Lindley ... his side got to grips with a difficult situation early on, and though they escaped twice when Peter Taylor hit shots against the woodwork, overall, United deserved their point.'

'The players were talking a lot more out on the field and the dressing room after the game was like it used to be,' smiled Lindley. 'The lads are analysing the match and talking about the things that went right and those that went wrong ... You cannot go on losing at home. We had to get something from this match and we did. One point is the start and the hope is now that we can build on that.'

And the man who would be leading that building soon became evident with the board leaking the story that its preferred candidate was the club's former England striker Allan Clarke.

After Clarke left Elland Road in 1978, a promising spell at Fourth Division Barnsley showcased his managerial qualities. Player-manager Clarke led the Tykes to promotion at the first attempt before retiring as a player to concentrate full-time on management as he sought to consolidate at the higher level.

Barnsley had begun the season well and after six games were a point off the top of the Third Division, but Clarke was flattered by the interest from Elland Road. The Barnsley board gave him permission to talk with Leeds.

'Before I met Manny Cussins, my assistant, Martin Wilkinson, produced a dossier for me on the current Leeds side, who were lying second bottom of the First Division. A big rebuilding job was required to make Leeds a force again. I'd need six players. I was offered £2 million to spend; it wasn't a fortune. Brian Clough had just spent £1 million on Birmingham City's Trevor Francis but it would enable me to buy three good players to begin with. I agreed to become Leeds United's new manager.'

No one could accuse Clarke of lacking confidence. As a player, he had always displayed a touch of arrogance, a confidence in his own abilities that characterised all great goalscorers. And Clarke – 'the true heir to Jimmy Greaves' – was certainly a great goalscorer. In 273 league games for Leeds, he had scored 110 times, with a further 113 goals in 241 games for other clubs and ten in his criminally short England career of nineteen caps. Leicester and Leeds had each broken the British transfer record to sign him and he had twice won Man of the Match awards in FA Cup finals.

The confidence he carried as a player also characterised his managerial persona – in his first days as Leeds boss, Clarke proclaimed, 'I'm a winner', adding that he would consider himself a failure if he hadn't won a trophy by the end of his three-year contract at Elland Road.

In his first meeting with his players, many of whom had played alongside him, Clarke assured them that there would be no favouritism and that there was plenty of time to pull clear of relegation. He was nevertheless scathing about the level of fitness, 'worse than that of the players I'd left at Barnsley'.

Leeds were an utter mess – the 3-0 defeat at Stoke in Adamson's final game had pitched them to the bottom of the table, with fifteen goals conceded in five games.

Clarke gave a warts-and-all interview to Vince Wilson of the *Sunday Mirror*, describing Leeds as a shambles. The article provoked a legal dispute between the club and Jimmy Adamson but all the controversy went over Clarke's head as he bullishly set about rebuilding confidence.

He stressed, like many other managers before him, the importance of building from the back. Entertainment was a luxury that could wait until the side was safe from relegation.

A goalless draw in his first game, at home to Manchester United on 20 September, went down well with the fans. It halted the protests and the complaints and got them back into the business of supporting the team.

It was a temporary honeymoon, a 4-1 defeat at Sunderland inflicting a heavy dose of reality, with Leeds simply not at the races. However, the results started to come and United resolutely clawed their way out of the relegation dogfight. First came a draw at Ipswich, then a 1-0 victory against Manchester City. Clarke used his column in the following programme to explain his intentions.

> Our league position at the moment dictates that results are by necessity more important than our performances ... I was pleased with the result and the two points although our overall performance was indifferent ... Having said that we kept a clean sheet and gave nothing away which was important in a match against a side struggling like ourselves.
>
> We are having difficulty at the moment putting away chances as our goals total suggests but if we are not conceding them at the other end then we are always in with a chance of picking up points.

Clarke's lack of attacking ambition was derided by rivals. Everton skipper Mike Lyons sneered that Leeds United were the most negative home side it had been his displeasure to play against. An unabashed Clarke simply pointed to the table as another 1-0 victory took Leeds up to 16th.

'I want to have the best eleven players in the country and the best club in the First Division. I have not got that, so I must utilise the players at my disposal in the best way I can,' retorted an unrepentant Clarke.

It appeared that Argentine midfielder Alex Sabella was getting the Clarke message, with Don Warters reporting in the *Yorkshire Evening Post*, 'His display against Everton was far more determined than some of his previous performances and, making allowance for a blatant penalty area dive, his overall showing was a definite plus sign for Clarke.'

The South American shaped the goal, playing Arthur Graham in down the wing. When a low cross came in, Sabella was onto it but miscued before Alan Curtis slid the ball home.

It was not all plain sailing, and Leeds lost four of their next five matches, with Arsenal running in five goals at Elland Road on 8 November.

Clarke had no excuses for the Arsenal debacle, telling the fans, 'We held a full and frank inquest into the game on Sunday morning when all the players reported to the ground. The pride of each and every one of us was deeply hurt on Saturday and if there was a Leeds player who did not feel some humiliation, then there's no place for that man at Elland Road.'

He acknowledged the 'magnificent support' of the fans and confirmed that he was ready to deal in the transfer market 'but they must be the right players and we must all be patient'.

Currying favour with the club's followers continued to be the order of the day. Clarke sought their views by way of a survey, asking why crowds were so low. The response rang clear and true: hooliganism and poor football were key issues. Excusing the latter as a necessary evil given the club's position, Clarke seized on the hooliganism issue with a rant about 'bringing back the birch' and suggestions that serious offenders should be thrashed in front of the main stand. He even offered his services to do some of the whipping.

Such populist outpourings smacked of learning at the knee of Margaret Thatcher or Norman 'Get On Your Bike' Tebbitt, a disconcerting feeling in a region where political leanings were largely left wing.

Paul Madeley's chronic knee problems were aggravated by a knock against Arsenal and the long-serving utility man accepted the inevitable and confirmed his retirement. The impact of his loss was cushioned by Clarke's insightful solution.

'I asked Eddie Gray to deputise in a twenty-minute practice match,' recalled Clarke. 'He was a revelation. I played him against Ipswich and he kept his place for the rest of the season. Eddie was brilliant in tandem with Arthur Graham and was by far the best left-back in the league. This decision extended his playing career by three seasons and it enabled me to revise my thoughts on who to purchase.'

Clarke's men steadied the ship with victory against Middlesbrough before stuttering to defeat at Southampton. A crowd of just 14,333 watched Leeds beat Brighton 1-0 at the end of November, the figure United's lowest for a league game since May 1963. Nevertheless, it was the first of three victories on the bounce as Clarke's men inched towards safety.

The third of those wins came against European Cup holders Nottingham Forest on 13 December. It was a turgid affair with most of the passing square or backwards and neither side prepared to take any risks. Then completely out of the blue came a goal when Brian Greenhoff thrashed in a stormer from 25 yards as the clock ran down. Peter Shilton could only watch in awe as it ballooned his net. 'I've never hit anything sweeter than that,' Greenhoff said of his first goal for Leeds.

The fans had to make the most of it. They would see United score only once more in the next six games, a penalty from Kevin Hird in an FA Cup third-round draw with Coventry. However, it was now the devil's own job to pierce the Leeds defence and two 1-0 victories, on 21 February at home to Sunderland and a week later at Old Trafford, saw them at the heady heights of twelfth in the table.

Victories away to Manchester United were a rare commodity; the winning goal scored by Brian Flynn would live long in the memory. It allowed those of a Leeds persuasion to play down the smash-and-grab nature of the game and just nod with satisfaction towards the scoreboard. The Red Devils were twice denied by the woodwork and Leeds had to thank John Lukic for a succession of last-ditch saves. They could crow in satisfaction, however, that Manchester United had failed to score against them in either league game. For Allan Clarke, it was only the points that mattered in his attritional pursuit of top-flight survival – everything else was irrelevant.

With fears of relegation formally dismissed on 4 April by a 3-0 defeat of Coventry, Leeds finished the season with the 'flourish' of conceding just two goals in their final eight matches. Both came in a 2-0 defeat at Brighton on 2 May, which was enough to ensure the Seagulls' own survival.

Clarke's pragmatism saw Leeds through to ninth, a remarkable finish after such a dismal autumn. Leaving aside the thrashings by Sunderland and Arsenal, a mere twenty-six goals had been conceded in thirty-four matches with clean sheets registered on nineteen occasions. The real story was at the other end of the field, however; Leeds players had managed a paltry thirty-four goals during Clarke's thirty-six games in charge. It was barren stuff, but the supporters consoled themselves with the notion that survival would prompt a more ambitious outlook.

CHAPTER THREE

Good Riddance to Bad Rubbish

'Everybody will get a fair chance' Allan Clarke told the players when he arrived at Elland Road in September 1980 before he realised how deep-set the club's issues were. Even before Christmas he was forced to redefine the statement, stung into action by United's lack of form. Singling out record £400,000 signing Alan Curtis as a man who did not fit his vision, Clarke sold him back to former club Swansea for a cut-price £165,000. That money and more was used to bring old favourite Frankie Gray back from Nottingham Forest in the summer. In each case, the player's value had plummeted since their original move, highlighting the vagaries of the transfer market. The same could not be said of Clarke's next deal.

Everyone knew that Leeds' priority was a proven goalscorer, so it came as a shock to everyone when Clarke signed England winger Peter Barnes. He was hardly a twenty-goal a season man, yet West Brom demanded and were paid £930,000, a fee widely derided as exorbitant.

Clarke thought that he had enough money still in the bank to add a hit man, particularly after raising £120,000 from the sale of Alex Sabella to Estudiantes and another £40,000 when Jeff Chandler went to Bolton. Barnes was signed to provide the ammunition for others and Clarke set his sights on Tony Woodcock and Gary Thompson. Each player would have cost less than Barnes and Clarke was confident of landing one of them. He was stopped in his tracks, however, when the board told him that the deals for Gray and Barnes had emptied the cupboard. Clarke was far from pleased, left with a lopsided squad that lacked any sort of cutting edge.

Clarke talked a good fight even if he feared the worst, which is certainly what he and Leeds got on the opening day of the 1982/83 season. As he took his squad to face promoted Swansea, the talk was all of a push for Europe. By the time they left South Wales, everyone knew that such ambitions were hopelessly overegged. Leeds returned to Yorkshire after suffering an emphatic 5-1 defeat. They had started with some promise, fighting back to equalise through Derek Parlane after an early concession, but were simply blown away at the start of the second half by a nine-minute hat-trick from Bob Latchford. Inevitably, Alan Curtis finished off the scoring with a flourish, revelling in the discomfiture of his old club.

As they travelled home, the players felt as jaundiced as their yellow kits, the second strip used because of a colour clash. The plain-look shirt was on its final knockings.

Ever since Liverpool signed their shirt sponsorship deal with Hitachi in 1979, clubs had been falling over themselves to cash in on the advertising market and Leeds had finally followed suit. Winder Power, an obscure, Pudsey-based manufacturer of electrical transformers, paid United £40,000 to become the club's first main shirt sponsor. As a reward, its RFW logo was featured on the breast of pinstriped, new-look shirts.

Blatant advertising such as this was not yet allowed in televised games. The scheduled broadcast of an Aston Villa-Brighton fixture a year earlier was cancelled when both teams refused to play without the names of sponsors on their shirts. The TV coverage of Leeds' game at Swansea meant that United's new kit was kept under wraps until the midweek game with Everton.

Attracted by the first chance to get a look at Barnes, a crowd of 26,502 brought a positive, if apprehensive, atmosphere to Elland Road. Clarke dropped both his full-backs, annoyed that Kevin Hird and Frank Gray had offered no protection against Swansea's wide men. There was little improvement. An overstretched Trevor Cherry failed to prevent a centre from the right after eleven minutes and Alan Biley fired home from 10 yards.

Leeds shook the sleep from their eyes and forced themselves into the game, conjuring up an equaliser after thirty-three minutes. Barnes did the business down the left and his cross to the back post was perfectly placed for Parlane to nod back into the danger zone. Arthur Graham was on it in an instant, snatching his first goal since December from a couple of yards out.

Graham's No. 11 shirt had been stolen by Peter Barnes, but the effervescent Scot proved his value on the right flank with some dangerous runs. Watching Scotland manager Jock Stein was suitably impressed. A hard-fought second half saw both teams hit the woodwork – the 1-1 draw was a fair outcome.

Graham took stage centre in the following game, netting a blistering hat-trick to see off Wolves. The result prompted some to dismiss the Swansea debacle as a blip, but four defeats from the next five games sent United tumbling to the bottom of the table. There were 4-0 losses at Coventry and Manchester City, the team all over the place and Barnes looking an expensive mistake. Reverses at Manchester United and Liverpool deepened the misery.

Clarke continued to look like a strong and sure-footed leader, but it had become clear that the squad at his disposal was simply not strong enough. It lacked both backbone and flair and no one had a clue what to do to halt its descent.

Only the paucity of the other sides milling round the foot of the table offered any hope that Leeds could dig their way out of this hole. They were playing poorly, their shortcomings badly exposed. Leaving aside Graham's treble against Wolves, United's goal tally after eleven games stood at four. How they ached for a man with the gifts of Clarke at his peak.

Barnes was certainly not that player, a fey, whimsical talent who could only fully contribute if the side's play was rebuilt around his style – Clarke could not countenance such a transformation. Barnes was no team man, unprepared to dig in when the going got tough. It was evident that he was a liability in what had become a difficult season. The crowd made their opinions painfully apparent and Barnes had to kick his heels for weeks in the stiffs.

'On his day he could be brilliant,' recalled Clarke. 'However, the game was changing and part of his role was to help out in defence, but he rarely did. During the season I dropped him. The board then interfered and demanded I play him, but I refused till he justified his place.'

The increase in reward for victory from two points to three was an innovation by the Football League which took some getting used to. Leeds were grateful beneficiaries when two wins in a week, against West Brom and Sunderland, allowed them to climb out of the relegation spots in October. The improvement coincided with the £400,000 purchase of Nottingham Forest hard man Kenny Burns, who formed a decent partnership in the centre of defence with Paul Hart.

Clarke dropped the inconsistent Parlane to make way for nineteen-year-old Aidan Butterworth. He scored in a 2-1 defeat at Nottingham Forest and again to beat Notts County as Leeds were suddenly up to the heady heights of sixteenth in early November. Had the manager found an unheralded saviour?

For a while it seemed so: following a 4-0 hammering at Southampton, a five-game unbeaten run gave fresh heart and the comfort of fourth spot by mid-January. The table was tight, however, and Leeds were ensnared in one of the closest relegation battles for years. The confidence they had built was brittle and they fell apart as fortunes turned again – Leeds went without a goal for seven games, the spell yielding a single point as they slipped back to 19th.

Fully appreciating the acuity of United's plight, Clarke gambled Leeds' entire future on an outrageous move for veteran Birmingham showman Frank Worthington. He was forced into offering promising Welsh defender Byron Stevenson in a straight trade – it was not a swap he welcomed but desperate times call for desperate measures and Clarke was desperate.

Worthington had a heartening start – he scored in his second game, a surprise victory at Sunderland, and added further goals against Forest and Notts County. He was no miracle worker, however, and after the success at Roker Park, Leeds won just once in nine attempts. A 4-3 defeat at West Ham in late April pitched them deep into trouble with only Middlesbrough keeping them off bottom spot.

Just as everything seemed at its darkest, Worthington scored another brace to inspire a 4-1 victory at Aston Villa. Villa had taken the lead, only for Graham to equalise from 20 yards as half-time beckoned. United exploded into the second period, netting three times inside fourteen minutes. The home side's attention was on their imminent European Cup final against Bayern Munich, but the story was about Leeds finding their form rather than any Villa collapse.

The game saw Barnes play the best football of his ill-fated stay at Elland Road. 'Peter produced one of the best performances I have ever seen from any Leeds player,' recalled Eddie Gray. 'With his explosive pace and ability on the ball, he was unstoppable that night.'

While the blistering victory saw United climb to seventeenth, their buffer down to the relegation spots was a single point. They could have eased their fears on 1 May with the visit of Stoke City, two places below them in the table and having played a game more. The supporters remained unconvinced that Leeds could do the business when it really mattered – fewer than 18,000 witnessed United display all their old shortcomings, bereft of ideas in a dismal goalless draw.

Crowds were fluctuating wildly – Leeds could pull in 30,000-plus crowds for big opponents like Liverpool and Manchester United, but there were eight games where attendances dropped below 20,000. The plunge in income was badly felt as Leeds headed for a £1.6 million loss. The overdraft soared by £1.2 million, pushing interest costs up to almost £200,000. This was a club heading rapidly south in every respect.

Defeats at Everton and Spurs looked to have sealed United's fate, but a sudden lifeline came their way when relegation rivals West Brom lost 3-0 at home to Manchester United. Leeds moved above them with a 3-3 draw at Birmingham, but it was a missed opportunity. A win would have seen Leeds overtake the Blues and climb into sixteenth position.

It could easily have been worse – a Worthington penalty five minutes from the end had been needed to secure the point.

With a couple of games left, Middlesbrough and Wolves were all but doomed, but the five teams above them were separated by just three points. With Leeds yet to face relegation rivals West Brom, it was too close to call.

The cause seemed lost when Leeds fell behind at home to Brighton a few days later, but on an emotion-draining day they enjoyed a final hurrah. With the clock ticking down, midfielder Gary Hamson hammered in the equaliser from fully 30 yards and then Kevin Hird squirmed his way through the Brighton defence to snatch victory from the jaws of defeat.

Elsewhere, Albion had won at Notts County but Stoke lost to Manchester United and were suddenly the side in trouble, level on points with West Brom and one below Leeds.

Allan Clarke celebrated in front of the Leeds fans as if he had won the title – at that moment everyone believed United were safe.

They had one game left, away to Albion, and a point in hand on both West Brom and Stoke, who would meet in the final game. A Leeds draw at The Hawthorns would be enough to guarantee safety.

The FA inflicted a grievous wound on United as the game approached. Worthington was controversially suspended, having reached twenty disciplinary points. Despite being on the same number of points, QPR defender Terry Fenwick was let off with a warning, clearing him to play in the FA Cup final. Railing against the injustice of it all, fans muttered darkly of conspiracy as they travelled south.

'I'm very upset about this, the verdicts are not consistent,' said Leeds' assistant manager Martin Wilkinson. 'How can the FA suspend a player for 20 points and let off a player with 20 points who has also been sent off?'

Clarke added, 'West Bromwich have had Cyrille Regis and Garry Owen sent off in the past two weeks. Because suspensions start two weeks after sendings off, or the last bookable offence, these two are available for vital matches. Worthington has taken all season to top 20 points, but we lose him under suspension. That's hardly fair.'

The fates were against Leeds – their worst performance of the season made it all too easy for an Albion side on top form. The Midlanders were emphatic 2-0 winners. In a vain attempt to get the match abandoned, the Leeds fans broke down the fences and stormed the pitch. The referee was too street smart to fall for that one and at the end Leeds were well beaten, knowing that they were almost certainly done for.

There remained the faintest of hopes – if Albion could win at Stoke in the remaining game, Leeds might yet be saved.

Disgruntled by the damage caused by United fans at The Hawthorns, Albion simply never looked like they would do Leeds any favours; Stoke's 3-0 victory formalised Leeds' relegation.

Clarke was at the Victoria Ground to witness the end, hoping against hope for a miracle but knew long before the end that there was to be no great escape. There were few tears shed by other clubs or the powers that be at United's demotion – the hooliganism that dogged Leeds like a bad smell had made the club a pariah. The riot in West Bromwich had been the final straw; when Leeds United came to town, everybody suffered.

Of course, that included United's own fans, at the end of their tether with the seemingly endless descent. It was only seven years since Revie's men had been in the European Cup final, and now here they were, facing the prospect of Second Division football after eighteen years in the top tier.

Clarke was a real glutton for punishment – he was all for carrying on, determined to bring Leeds back up at the first time of asking. He was denied the opportunity to do so, the board showing him the door in the summer.

They might have relented had Clarke not chosen to fly out to Portugal rather than attend meetings with the bank to discuss United's finances.

According to director Bill Fotherby, 'The manager was vital because he had to put values on players. Manny [Cussins] had to say, "I'm sorry, the manager will not be coming, he's on holiday."'

Fotherby claimed that only he and vice-chairman Leslie Silver voted to allow Clarke to keep his job when the board considered the position.

Clarke took the decision with dignity and re-emerged at the start of 1983 as Scunthorpe manager, leading them within weeks to promotion from the Third Division.

CHAPTER FOUR

Into the Wilderness

Leeds United's exile to the wilderness lasted far longer than the forty days Jesus Christ spent in the desert. For them, years of torment lay ahead.

Relegation after nine grisly months of shapeless football, plummeting attendances and fractious relationships between players saw them contemplating a future that included Rotherham, Grimsby, Carlisle, Barnsley and Shrewsbury rather than Liverpool, Manchester United and Arsenal. But the demise had been coming for years, taking root when Tony Currie was sold in 1979.

Jimmy Adamson never got to grips with the challenge and was driven out of Elland Road by an unforgiving fan base. Allan Clarke fared no better than Adamson and paid the price for the drop with his job, the directors unconvinced that he and his management team had the experience needed to handle the challenge.

It was bizarre that the man they selected to take up the cudgels had even less of a managerial record.

Eddie Gray, by his own admission, was 'the most convenient option ... I was never under any illusions about why Leeds chose me. It had a lot to do with the fact that the club were in financial trouble ... I was already being paid £25,000 a year as a player and managerial responsibilities meant Leeds having to fork out only an extra £5,000.'

'Financial trouble' was an understatement – the club's overdraft was nudging £2 million. Already trading at a loss, things were set to get even tighter with gate receipts plummeting as a result of relegation. The directors were forced to cover the borrowings with personal guarantees, much to their displeasure.

To mitigate the financial stress, the club threw the doors of Elland Road open to homeless Hunslet Rugby League Club. Their usage of the stadium would yield United £1,000 per game. It might have made financial sense but the move had repercussions for a playing surface that was notoriously poor, often mudbound as a result of the archaic drains. Even if Leeds had the best players in the country, they would have struggled to show their class on a pitch that often resembled a beach.

Gray put together a management team in double-quick time. Close friend Jimmy Lumsden, a former teammate from the old days, came in as assistant manager and Gray persuaded Manchester United youth coach Syd Owen to return to Elland Road as chief scout. Owen had been one of Don Revie's key lieutenants in the 1960s and 1970s but had moved on when Revie took the England job.

Gray's immediate priority was stabilising the finances rather than getting the club back up to the First Division. Reducing costs by getting the big earners off the books was a necessary evil. 'The board tried, unsuccessfully, to persuade certain players to take a wage cut,' recalled Gray. 'At one point I can remember Inland Revenue representatives coming to the ground to claim some of the tax we owed by taking away the club cars.'

Getting rid of players was a challenge – there were few who had any value on the market, especially given the size of their contracts. Initially, the only man for whom Gray could find a buyer was Carl Harris, off to Charlton for a bargain £100,000. Eventually, he managed to get Peter Barnes and Derek Parlane off an exorbitant wage bill with season-long loans in Spain and Hong Kong.

The failure to move players on hit the directors in the pocket but at least meant that Leeds were competitive in the early weeks. There was one notable absentee in Gary Hamson. He required a cartilage operation after a bad injury in the final game of the relegation season and figured just once all year. It was unfortunate; after taking a while to get his Elland Road career moving, he had made himself a mainstay of Allan Clarke's midfield.

Gray sanctioned the departure of a promising Yorkshire-born goalkeeper, eighteen-year-old David Seaman, seeing no way of keeping him happy as reserve to John Lukic. A £5,000 fee took the youngster to Peterborough and a future that brought worldwide fame with Arsenal and England.

It was an error of judgement. Before the end of the season, Lukic had requested a transfer, prompting Gray to persuade old stager David Harvey to forsake his new life in Canada for a return to Elland Road. Terry Connor accompanied Lukic out of the club, swapped in a player-exchange deal for Brighton's Andy Ritchie.

The fans were devastated when Connor, one of their own, checked out, but Gray was desperate for someone who could get the best out of the other players. 'The similarities between Aidan [Butterworth] and Terry inevitably mitigated against their chances of forging an effective partnership,' he said. 'It was difficult for us to keep the ball in the opposing half, and the impression of our attack being too lightweight was further underlined ... By March, it was obvious that we needed someone who could give us a better blend in this area, someone who could hold the ball up and set up chances for players in other positions. Brighton's Andy Ritchie seemed ideal. Unfortunately, we could only get him in a part-exchange deal involving Terry.'

Gray shamelessly pinned the club's future on youth, taking a leaf from Don Revie's book. Connor, Lukic, Butterworth, Gwyn Thomas and Martin Dickinson had all come through the ranks and in his first season Gray gave opportunities to John Sheridan, Neil Aspin, Mark Gavin, Tommy Wright and Scott Sellars. He also bought in twenty-year-old midfielder John Donnelly, signed for £85,000 from Dumbarton in March. It was the first time that Gray felt in a position to spend, so tight were the finances.

Gray had asked for £65,000 to make permanent the loan of Neil McNab from Brighton but the board rejected the move for lack of funds. The cash to finance the Donnelly deal was generated by a run in the FA Cup.

Gray shaped his side around a core of old stagers: Paul Hart, Kevin Hird, Arthur Graham, brother Frank and himself. He coaxed a decent season out of the squad, though they were crippled by an inability to win games – too many points were frittered away, half the games ending in draws.

Leeds peaked at fifth after three victories on the bounce as March moved into April, but a return of one victory from the remaining nine games saw them slip to an underwhelming eighth, ten points off the promotion places.

The season was scarred by the appalling behaviour of fans frustrated at having to deal with United's fall from grace. A succession of incidents saw the club's name dragged through the mud.

The United board were left in no doubt by the authorities about the severity of their anger after the grim scenes at The Hawthorns in May 1982. Painfully aware of the thinness of the ice on which they stood, the directors feared the worst after the opening game of the new season, away to Grimsby. Some supporters went on what *The Sun* termed 'an orgy of drinking, looting and fighting' in Cleethorpes, where 600 Leeds fans stayed the night before the match. They caused damage at Grimsby's Blundell Road ground as trouble flared once again. Despite warnings of fines and possible closure of the stadium, there were clashes with Chelsea fans and a ball-bearing attack on Kevin Keegan and other Newcastle players.

The first day victory secured at Grimsby marked the start of a five-game unbeaten spell which took Leeds up to fifth. Fulham blew them apart in the following match but confidence was restored by three exciting clashes with Newcastle.

Two of the games came in the second round of the League Cup. Newcastle seemed to have done the hard job with a 1-0 victory in the first leg at Elland Road, but they caught a cold at St James' Park.

The night started poorly and Leeds' hopes looked slim after Jeff Clarke gave Newcastle the lead within ninety seconds, volleying through John Lukic's legs.

An unlikely revival was sparked when Newcastle defender Wes Saunders, under pressure from Aidan Butterworth, turned Arthur Graham's cross into his own net after thirty-two minutes. Frank Worthington, in one of his final games for Leeds, tied the aggregate score with twenty minutes to go, diving to head home a cross from Eddie Gray.

Leeds went into extra-time knowing that if there were no more scores their away goals would see them through, but there was no inclination to sit on their advantage.

Lukic somehow saved a point-blank Keegan header to keep Leeds' heads above water and the first period of the extra thirty ended with no further goals.

Gray took himself off at the break and introduced Terry Connor. Within seven minutes of his arrival, the nineteen-year-old combined with Worthington to lay on an open goal for twenty-year-old Butterworth. A minute from the end, Connor settled the outcome himself when he chipped goalkeeper Kevin Carr.

For Trevor Cherry, who left a month later to take over as player-manager at Bradford City, it was a fitting way to say goodbye – getting the better of former England captain Keegan meant a lot to him.

'I roomed with Kevin for a couple of years and knew him quite well from our England days. Me and Kevin got on really well and we had the same sort of background. In the early days with England, his wife used to drop him off at Huddersfield and my wife used to drive us through to Manchester when we'd be flying out of there on England duty. He was a great lad.'

Three days later, Newcastle and Leeds met a third time, in the league at Elland Road. It was first blood to Newcastle with full-back John Anderson on hand to make sure when a Chris Waddle cross was fumbled by Lukic. Leeds bit back instantly; Frank Gray's shot was deflected by a defender, setting up a chance for Worthington on the 6-yard line. He headed home bravely despite Kenny Wharton's swinging boot.

Connor came on as second-half sub and turned the game again. He set up Kenny Burns to score within four minutes of entering the fray. Butterworth notched a third with six minutes to go as Leeds consolidated sixth spot and opened an eight-point gap on Newcastle.

'Considering we had to fight back from behind the other night and play extra-time and that we had to do it again today, this has been a most satisfying win for me,' said Eddie Gray at the end. 'In fact, I think the three games that we have played in October against Newcastle have been among the most exciting in which I have taken part.'

The evening was marred by more crowd trouble with two Newcastle players hit by metal missiles thrown from the crowd. Keegan was felled after being struck on the head, as he had been in the first of the League Cup games. Referee Malcolm Heath stopped the game and ordered both teams from the field. When play restarted, Anderson was also hit, although it was claimed that the missile, thrown by a Newcastle supporter, was meant for Frank Worthington. The teams were taken off again for a brief spell and later in the game there were scuffles among fans.

The consequences for Leeds were grim. On 6 November, the front page of United's programme carried a grim warning:

> The future of Leeds United Association Football Club hangs in the balance. This in no way exaggerates the position and must not be taken as an idle threat. Despite repeated pleas and warnings, the mindless actions of a minority of the club's so-called followers last Saturday have placed an enormous degree of uncertainty over this great club ... We would ask for the help and cooperation of everyone who have Leeds United at heart – and we appreciate that this is the majority of our supporters – to help rid the club of the 'scab' element who, although small in numbers, have caused the club so many problems and whose loathsome actions now place the very existence of Leeds United in jeopardy.

Leeds were on notice that their place in the Football League itself could be under threat. The FA ordered the directors to close the Elland Road terraces for two games and impose all-ticket conditions. Consequently, the attendance for the QPR game was a dismal 11,528, the lowest for a league game since May 1963. The crowd for the following fixture against Shrewsbury was even smaller, at 8,741. One had to go back to February 1962 for a lower figure.

The players were undeterred, even though they were now without the departed Brian Flynn, Worthington and Cherry. They maintained a place in the top ten for most of the season, although they never got close enough to really suggest they could get promotion at the first time of asking.

They also enjoyed a high-profile FA Cup marathon against mighty Arsenal. After seeing Preston off 3-0 in the third round, Leeds performed well in the first game at Highbury. They held out for a 1-1 draw after taking the lead when Connor harried Arsenal midfielder Peter Nicholas into putting the ball past goalkeeper Pat Jennings.

The midweek replay at Elland Road was ruined by storms. The wind was so strong that asbestos sheeting was ripped from the roof of the Lowfields Road stand, leading to closure of part of that side.

The pitch, heavily sanded and showing the effects of Hunslet's use, was poor, making football a lottery. There was little surprise when normal time ended without a goal.

The conditions made for excitement in the closing seconds of extra-time as tiring players on both sides made mistakes. With a minute left, Leeds broke swiftly out of defence and stormed down the left flank. Connor evaded Stewart Robson and fired low across the area. Butterworth, his socks around his ankles, had barely enough energy to force the ball home. Crippled by cramp, he struggled to get back into his own half for the restart.

Still there was time for Arsenal to equalise, England international Graham Rix catching the United wall unprepared as he curled home a free kick.

Victory had been in United's grasp – they sank to the sodden turf in despair at seeing the glory snatched away.

A second replay was scheduled for the following Monday at Highbury after Arsenal won the toss to determine home advantage. It was delayed for forty-eight hours because of the state of the pitch. The game was finally played out on a bitterly cold evening with the first half ruined by snow, though United were boosted by the recall of John Sheridan.

The Gunners got their noses in front after the break – they had already seen one goal chalked off for offside and now England striker Tony Woodcock turned in the area and shot past Lukic. It was the first time that Arsenal had been ahead in the marathon and still they could not shake Leeds off.

After seventy minutes, United were back in it. Sheridan had already gone close on two occasions and Leeds sprang forward again after Lukic saved one-handed from Vladimir Petrovic. Arthur Graham's floated shot from 30 yards looked on its way in until Pat Jennings got his fingers to it and touched onto the crossbar. Connor reacted quickest and seized on the opportunity to equalise. With eight minutes of the game left, Rix settled matters, firing home from 20 yards after being set up by Woodcock.

The way his boys had risen to the challenge fully justified Gray's faith in them and gave manager and directors confidence that they could launch a genuine promotion push the following season.

CHAPTER FIVE

Ringing the Changes

By the summer of 1983, Leeds United chairman Manny Cussins was seventy-seven and bowed down by United's chronic financial problems. Eddie Gray's failure to achieve promotion at the first attempt had added to the woes, confirming that the revival of United's fortunes would not be an overnight thing. Cussins simply did not have the strength in him to lead the fight.

The paucity of attendances in Leeds' first season back in the Second Division meant that the club required directors' loans of £130,000, net transfer outgoings of £321,000 and donations of £205,000 to stay afloat. How long Leeds could keep their heads above water in this most dismal of divisions was anybody's guess.

Such matters were behind Cussins' thinking when he brought in London-born paint entrepreneur Leslie Silver as vice-chairman in 1981 and he now began paving the way for Silver to assume the chair.

Silver's investment was badly needed, but every bit as important was the vigour he brought with him. Vigour was a quality that Bill Fotherby also had in abundance.

Fotherby had become a close friend of Silver, the two becoming stalwarts of the 100 Club, the body populated by the great and good of Leeds and dedicated to raising funds for the club.

Fotherby had long coveted a seat on the United board and resented the fact that Silver got there first. He had been a devout fan from an early age, unlike Arsenal-supporting Silver.

Fotherby, a motormouth, natural-born salesman, was larger than life and twice as loud, making himself a rich man running a local clothing firm. Few who came across the eccentric teller of tall tales would forget him, an engaging lover of life and doer of deals.

Over the years he had bought up considerable numbers of club shares. His scheming to gain a seat on the board was thwarted by Cussins, who never trusted him, deeming him a troublemaker.

Eventually, Fotherby managed to wear Cussins down and was offered a position on the board, an invitation which helped transform the club.

'From that day I joined,' recalled Fotherby, 'I made a difference at Leeds United. I changed Leeds United. I wanted success, I wanted what every supporter at Leeds United wanted … I knew I'd bring life to it. We needed money, and I was commercial; my job was to bring money into Leeds United and get us publicity, because what were Leeds? Who were Leeds? Don Revie had gone and they'd had that tremendous, tremendous success. How do you follow that?'

Fotherby quickly became established as Silver's right-hand man, pushed constantly by him as a go between to bridge the gap between manager and board. Eddie Gray was never keen on getting involved in such shenanigans, preferring to deal directly with the chairman.

And there was plenty of dealings in the summer of 1983. Disappointingly, however, they were all about pruning the payroll and ridding the club of big earners, including John Lukic off to Arsenal for £125,000, Arthur Graham (Manchester United £50,000) and Paul Hart (Nottingham Forest £40,000). The sums might have been depressingly small – even less was realised from the free transfers of Kenny Burns to Derby and Brian Greenhoff to Rochdale.

Gray invested the money in the Scottish market, bringing in Celtic striker George McCluskey (£161,000) and Aberdeen midfielder Andy Watson (£60,000). As part of the balancing of the books, Gray later shipped Derek Parlane out to Manchester City for £160,000 and Gwyn Thomas to Barnsley for £40,000. The return from Spain of Peter Barnes bolstered the squad, while Gray also recruited a fellow Leeds legend, thirty-seven-year-old Peter Lorimer, to bring experience to midfield.

Lorimer's maturity was desperately needed, with Gray forced to rely increasingly on youngsters like Martin Dickinson (a veteran at twenty), John Stiles (ninteen), Neil Aspin, John Sheridan (both eighteen), and seventeen-year-olds Denis Irwin, Scott Sellars and Tommy Wright. There was a fresh-faced look to the Leeds squad, something that appealed to the fans, but a huge gamble on youth alone was a high-risk strategy.

The knockout competitions offered an opportunity to earn enough money to fund further recruitment but Leeds did badly, losing 4-1 at Third Division Oxford in the fourth round of the League Cup and then to Allan Clarke's Scunthorpe United (also of Division Three) at the first hurdle in the FA Cup.

Fortunes were no better in the league with six defeats from the first nine games. The appalling run pitched Gray's men into the bottom four, the writing on the wall right from an opening day defeat at home to Newcastle.

Gray had included Barnes, McCluskey and Watson, but a Newcastle team containing Kevin Keegan and Chris Waddle was far too strong to withstand.

There was a complete absence of any attacking threat – even when goalkeeper Kevin Carr was injured at the start of the second half, forcing Waddle to take over in goal, Leeds could not take advantage. Waddle was virtually redundant after donning the gloves.

The match was lost to a twenty-second-minute curler from John Anderson – deflected by Martin Dickinson, it flew past David Harvey. The Leeds keeper was forced into two excellent saves by substitute Ken Wharton as Newcastle underlined their dominance.

Gray kept the players locked in the dressing room for an hour after the match, laying down the law. He left them in no doubt as to the unacceptability of their performance, accusing them of letting down the fans – a crowd of 30,806 had flocked to Elland Road only to have all their expectations for the season smothered.

A 5-1 hammering at Shrewsbury Town on 1 October was just as hard to take. There were few positives to take from a game that Leeds simply threw away. For the third game running they took the lead through Andy Ritchie only to collapse in the second half.

They improved sufficiently to beat Cambridge and then won 2-0 at Barnsley to edge up to thirteenth. There was a dear price to pay – the broken leg suffered by John Sheridan sidelined him until the following August.

Losing their midfield playmaker knocked the stuffing out of Leeds. Gray's back-to-the-future solution was to seek out Lorimer. After signing in December, the Scot made his first appearance on New Year's Eve as sub for two-goal George McCluskey in a 4-1 defeat of Middlesbrough. It was more than twenty-one years since Lorimer's first debut for Leeds but he settled to his new station remarkably well, taking the club captaincy and directing a revival in United's fortunes.

Despite the contributions of McCluskey and Lorimer, the star of the day was seventeen-year-old Scottish youth international Tommy Wright. His 'chirpy confidence ... pointed a beacon of hope in Leeds United's fight to avoid the Division', gushed the *Yorkshire Evening Post*. Wright, who had scored in two defeats over Christmas, played a key role in United's first four-goal performance in the league since they won 4-1 at Aston Villa in April 1982.

Wright was an unexpected rallying point after the dismissal of Martin Dickinson seven minutes after the break for elbowing Paul Sugrue in the face. Leeds were two ahead at the time and there were fears that Middlesbrough would exploit their man advantage, but Wright had an inspired afternoon, leading the Boro defence a sorry dance. He was a constant thorn in their flesh and was denied what looked like a goal when the referee adjudged that the ball had not crossed the goal line, though it clearly came back out off the stanchion.

Far from being frustrated, Wright simply upped his work rate and with seventy minutes on the clock found himself in the clear after a long clearance by David Harvey. He ignored the pleas of two teammates in the middle and smashed an angled shot in off the far post.

'For a seventeen-year-old he has a lot of composure,' beamed Gray. 'Regardless of the number of chances missed, he has the confidence in his ability to try again.'

Leeds drew three days later at Manchester City and then won five league games on the bounce. Burgeoning hopes that there might be a late entry into the promotion stakes were dashed by a six-game winless spell as March ran into April, though any fears of relegation had long been dispelled.

Leeds might not have figured in the final promotion shake-up but they had a part to play in the outcome – the final six weeks of the season saw them in action against the three sides who went up.

First came third-placed Newcastle at St James' Park on 28 March. The home XI was star-studded, boasting past and future England internationals Keegan, Waddle, Terry McDermott and Peter Beardsley, but Leeds matched them punch for punch. The only goal of the game came after twenty-five minutes, headed past his own keeper by Denis Irwin. Truth be known, Leeds never looked likely to equalise.

It was a tighter game three days later when Leeds hosted Howard Wilkinson's Sheffield Wednesday, second in the table. Leeds were in charge for almost all the first half, Wednesday took control in the second, but it seemed certain that the two Yorkshire sides would simply cancel each other out. The final ten minutes brought the decisive moments of the game and most of the excitement. Tony Cunningham wriggled free of Neil Aspin's afternoon-long attentions to head Gavin Oliver's cross from the left-back through a crowded penalty area for Gary Bannister to poke in his twentieth goal of the season.

Stewards were still clearing one spectator from the field as Gary Hamson put Scott Sellars away down the left and Andy Ritchie did the rest when the ball came in.

Wednesday keeper Martin Hodge was adamant that Ritchie had punched the ball into the net, but the striker denied the accusations. The referee took Ritchie's side and awarded a goal to tie the match.

On 5 May, Leeds lost 5-0 at Chelsea, old rivals on the way to the Second Division title. The game is infamous for the United fans' trashing of Stamford Bridge's electronic scoreboard after the concession of the fifth goal, prompting an outburst from Chelsea owner Ken Bates. 'I shall not rest until Leeds United are kicked out of the Football League. Their fans are the scum of the Earth, absolute animals and a disgrace. I will do everything in my power to make this happen.'

Bates never managed such a feat in his time at Chelsea but would come perilously close to doing so during his time at Leeds more than two decades later.

Lorimer had already scored the three goals he needed to bypass John Charles' club record of 153 in the league. The penalty he notched against Oldham on 24 April did the trick and secured a 2-0 victory. The pre-match headlines, though, had all been about Peter Barnes.

The former England winger had been transfer-listed but hinted that he might yet have a future at Elland Road when he scored a week earlier against Huddersfield. Gray had other ideas, dropping Barnes for the Oldham match to bring in twenty-year-old reserve Mark Gavin.

'Peter isn't injured,' explained Gray. 'He's been left out because I feel the youngster deserves a chance. Mark has played very well in the reserves and if I'd been him I'd have wondered why I wasn't in the first team. Now he has his chance.'

Gray's decision was vindicated by the victory, United's first in seven matches, and Gavin subsequently opened his Leeds account in a 3-0 defeat of Carlisle United.

Barnes never found the net for United again and left for Coventry City two months into the following campaign.

Lorimer added to his new club record with a goal in the penultimate game, helping secure the draw at Swansea that took United up to tenth. They confirmed the position a week later when Wright scored the only goal against Charlton. That fixture marked Eddie Gray's swansong as a player after almost 600 appearances in United colours.

It was sad to see such a wonderful player bid his farewell. Certainly, a few tears were shed that afternoon, but thirty-six-year-old Gray simply could no longer do full justice to two roles. It was more than eighteen years since he first appeared in the United first team, scoring in a 3-0 victory against Sheffield Wednesday on New Year's Day 1966.

CHAPTER SIX

A Tragic Season

With United's overdraft climbing stubbornly towards £1.6 million on the back of a loss of £123,000, Eddie Gray was left in no doubt that playing the market was not an option for him. Long hours of thought were required even about the £20,000 deal he struck for twenty-two-year-old Hartlepool central defender Andy Linighan. The player was seen as a straight replacement for Kenny Burns, who had left for Derby in February and the comparison between the two men gave evidence that Gray's ambitions were severely constrained by the financial reality besetting Elland Road.

All his other moves were either in the youth market (John Scales and Peter Swan) or free transfers (John Stiles from Vancouver Whitecaps) – these were gambler's punts on unproven talent in the hope that at least one would pay off.

Gray helped ease the financial position by getting two of his remaining high earners off the payroll, Kevin Hird departing for Burnley on a free transfer and Peter Barnes joining Coventry for £65,000.

The fans had to grit their teeth, though they could at least console themselves with the freshness and energy of youth. It was the best crop of talent to emerge in years and many harked back fondly to Don Revie's halcyon years. Gray was the ideal man to nurture such starlets. He had the happy knack of getting the best out of them and seemed to know exactly when they were ready for blooding. Somehow, though, they were never quite as good as Leeds needed to escape a difficult division.

The core of any 'normal' team would be in their twenties, but of the XI that started the opening game at Notts County there were four teenagers (Denis Irwin, Neil Aspin, John Sheridan and Tommy Wright) and two veterans (David Harvey and Peter Lorimer). Less than half were in the core range (Gary Hamson, Andy Watson, Andy Linighan, George McCluskey and Frank Gray) and Linighan was a complete novice at this level.

There was no way such a line-up could expect to be among the front-runners – in another couple of years maybe, but not yet. It was a frustrating time with many wondering whether Leeds could ever regain their 'rightful status' – they were becoming entrenched as a mid-table second-tier side and that was too grim a prospect to contemplate. A wonderful opening burst hinted at a decent season, but the team quickly fell away.

The supporters, the bitter core who remained loyal, relied on non-footballing pursuits to keep their spirits up, taking their irritation out on opposing supporters and the poor unfortunates in the towns they visited. The reputation of United's festering hooligan element always preceded them and they reacted badly when baited by rival fans.

At the start of his first full season as chairman, Leslie Silver appealed for the fans to refrain from any behaviour that would damage the club. His words had little impact and when United travelled to Grimsby in September, the scenes were eerily reminiscent of their 1982 visit.

Caroline Gall from *Service Crew* said: 'There were several arrests after fighting in the streets when the pubs shut, refusing to serve the lads anymore. Gangs were reportedly wandering along the High Street and surrounding roads armed with bricks and two lads were hit by a police car.'

The game itself produced a 2-0 victory, extending United's 100 per cent record to four games. Eighteen-year-old Tommy Wright was the catalyst for the success, netting five times in that spell and Gray and the fans began to ruminate over whether a corner had been turned. It could not continue and Leeds fell to three successive defeats.

Crowds had been edging up towards 20,000, but a cynical 'told you so' attitude saw just 14,290 present to welcome Oldham when they visited Elland Road on 29 September.

Undeterred, the Leeds players found some irrepressible football and blew the visitors to the four winds. With Peter Lorimer pulling the strings in midfield, Leeds took the lead after four minutes with Wright nodding home from a Lorimer cross. They took a while to add to their total but as soon as Andy Ritchie made it 2-0 in the second half, the brakes came off – Ritchie snaffled a hat-trick with Linighan and Sheridan breaking their ducks for the season to register a 6-0 victory.

Ritchie and Wright continued to plunder the goals; another hat-trick from the former was the deciding factor as Leeds beat Wimbledon 5-2 in December. United looked ideally placed for a promotion push and rose to fifth with a 2-0 victory at Wolves just before Christmas.

They slipped to defeat at Blackburn on Boxing Day, but their form and football alerted the media to the chances of an upset when Leeds came out of the hat with a plum home tie against First Division Everton in the FA Cup.

The match was switched to a Friday night and became the first ever game to be broadcast live from Elland Road.

This was a strong Everton side, boasting many of the players that had helped them win the trophy the previous May. Howard Kendall's men delivered a routine two-goal victory, though the publicity did 'gallant' Leeds a world of good.

Undeterred, Gray's boys continued to prosper in the Second Division, a hat-trick from Wright the cornerstone of a 5-0 thrashing of Notts County a fortnight later.

Impressed by United's staying power, Silver and the board saw fit to bolster, releasing money for Gray to strengthen, albeit only a whisker over £100,000. A delighted manager brought in Villa keeper Mervyn Day and Southampton striker Ian Baird. Both men upped Leeds' quality and would become United legends. The robust Baird scored six times in ten games and Day kept nine clean sheets in eighteen appearances.

Baird's debut goal came in a Monday evening victory at promotion-chasing Manchester City and five days later he added another in an exciting 4-1 hammering of Crystal Palace. John Sheridan contributed two goals, sealing victory with a 25-yard strike after eighty-three minutes.

Gray spelled out his ambitions at the end, telling the press, 'There are five games left and we must aim to win all of them.'

The momentum seemed to be with Leeds, but they drew two of their following four matches and their chances were tenuous as they prepared for their final game, away to Birmingham City on 11 May. The Blues had already confirmed their own promotion alongside Oxford but even if Leeds won, they would need Manchester City and Portsmouth to lose in order for them to go up. The other club still in the mix was Blackburn and victory for them would also finish Leeds' chances.

Right at the start of the season, the two clubs' hooligan element, the Service Crew at United and Birmingham's Zulu Warriors, had marked the end-of-season clash as the big one, the chance for a real ruck between two of the game's most feared firms. Plans had been laid and chaos was guaranteed.

Football was staggering under the fearsome yoke of hooliganism at the time, trouble plumbing new depths. The problem defied all that Margaret Thatcher's Conservative government could throw at it.

A couple of months earlier the Luton-Millwall FA Cup replay, televised live, gave a national audience first-hand evidence of the violence boiling away under the surface. The evening was brought to a sorry finale with a full-scale on-field confrontation between opposing fans.

As the *Football Whispers* website reported, 'The incident did nothing to help football's awful reputation at a time when football hooliganism was rife and footage of a rampaging mob running freely on a football pitch in front of millions of viewers at home would very much set the tone for the remainder of the season, if not the decade ... It was now football fans who were enemy number one after a series of tragic events meant that, for football, May 1985 would become the worst in living memory.'

And the Birmingham-Leeds fixture delivered violence of the worst kind – the afternoon ended with 500 injured and one dead.

There had been trouble in the crowd all afternoon with fighting and missiles thrown. At the final whistle, Birmingham hooligans, armed with broken plastic seating, bits of advertisement hoardings, iron stanchions, pieces of wood and glass bottles, poured onto the pitch and headed for the Leeds section. They set upon a hundred policemen, including seven mounted officers, who stood in their way. The horses were targeted, with one officer dragged from his mount and severely beaten. Within seconds, the police were struggling at both ends of the pitch.

Birmingham City manager Ron Saunders was dragged out to plead for reason and made a despairing appeal over the stadium's public address system, begging the crowd to disperse.

Penned into one corner of the arena, thugs responded with another charge towards the police, counter-attacking and throwing missiles at them, causing the alarmed horses to buck and rear.

Saunders' voice boomed from the Tannoy: 'In the name of football, please stop.' Gradually, the storm eased, but only after a police charge scattered the mob. Police had fought a running battle to keep the two sets of fans apart and during the subsequent inquiry, the scenes were described by Justice Popplewell as more like 'the Battle of Agincourt than a football match'. Hundreds were injured, including ninety-six policemen. Fifteen-year-old Leeds fan Ian Hambridge, attending his first game, wasn't as lucky.

Having fled the fighting, he took shelter behind a 12-foot wall at the back of the stadium. Undermined by the impact of the pitched battles, the wall crumbled and tumbled to the ground. The boy suffered fatal head injuries and died in Smethwick's Neurological Hospital less than twenty-four hours later.

That same afternoon, tragedy struck at Bradford City's Valley Parade stadium. Having clinched the Third Division title the week before, the fixture was seen as the perfect opportunity for the Bantams to celebrate promotion, but the game would be remembered for different, darker reasons.

At the end of the first half, a fire broke out in the main stand, due to be demolished in the summer. In less than four minutes, the blaze engulfed the structure with its highly flammable wooden roof. Burning embers fell from the roof onto the crowd below, while black smoke and flames soon enveloped the whole stand.

Most of the exits were locked as soon as the game started and there were no stewards present to open them. Fifty-six people died at Valley Parade that day, twenty-seven of them found by the exit at the rear of the stand, burned to death or killed by the thick black smoke which hung heavy across the city.

It was a dark day in a month that would end with English clubs banned from European competition after the mayhem caused by Liverpool supporters during the European Cup final against Juventus. Ten years earlier, the frustration of Leeds United fans spilled over against Bayern Munich in their Paris final. The 'infamy' of that episode was as nothing set against the thirty-nine deaths and 600 injured at Heysel.

CHAPTER SEVEN

The King Is Dead, Long Live the King

The disappointment of losing 1-0 at St Andrew's on the final day of the season was as nothing next to the rumblings provoked by the infamous riot that dominated the headlines. Leeds were once more branded pariahs, the leaders of thug culture. Even the deaths caused at Heysel by Liverpool fans and the part played in the riot by the Zulu Warriors presented no challenge to United's supremacy as the devils incarnate in the eyes of the public. Many self-appointed guardians of the ethical compass threw their hands up in despair and proclaimed themselves finished with football for good following the pitched battles in Birmingham. Eddie Gray and the directors of Leeds United were completely baffled by the course of events, at a loss as to what they could do to put an end to the hooliganism that dogged the club.

Football memories are short-lived, however, and the board and the manager could bask in the warming glow of the decent spell of form exhibited by Gray's youngsters in the spring. The quality and verve of their football saw them among the promotion favourites for the new season. Optimism was boosted by the £250,000 capture of Doncaster's midfield kingpin and captain Ian Snodin, who had impressed for England's Under-21 side. His arrival, following the recruitment of Mervyn Day and Ian Baird weeks earlier, confirmed Gray's intention to stiffen his squad's resolve for a real promotion push. The sale of brother Frank to Sunderland brought in £100,000, but the net outflow represented a major financial commitment by the board.

It was part of a grand scheme to make Leeds upwardly mobile but Leslie Silver was pilloried when he revealed how he intended to fund the programme of improvement. Groaning under the yoke of a £1.6 million bank overdraft and the annual interest of £157,000, Leeds were racking up large losses, only kept afloat by donations and player sales. By 1985 any player of value had been flogged off and even donations of £139,000 could not keep the wolf from the door. The £350,000 spent on Day, Baird and Snodin pushed the club to the edge.

Silver knew that drastic action was required to end the vicious cycle that beset the club and came up with a controversial solution – he negotiated the sale of the Elland Road stadium to the local council for £2.5 million, allowing the debt to be cleared at a stroke. The council granted the club a 125-year lease to use the stadium but selling off the family silver did not go down well with the supporters. How else Leeds could have afforded a talent like Snodin was anybody's guess, but the sale was hugely symbolic for the fans.

Silver hailed the sale as a 'kiss of life', protesting that it 'released the club from an intolerable burden of debt'. His words were greeted with cynicism and for a time he was one of the most hated men in the city.

Silver could tolerate the criticism, but dilution of his control over the football club was a high price to pay for solvency. As reward for their altruism, the council demanded a voice on the board – councillors Malcolm Bedford, Ronald Feldman and Alec Hudson were given seats at the boardroom table while Eric Carlile, secretary of the official Leeds United's Supporters' Club, represented the fans.

Carlile was a regular attender at United games, his first coming against York City in 1943, and widely respected by his peers. He became assistant secretary of the Supporters' Club in 1958 before taking on the secretary role later that year, a position he held for fifty years. Whether his appointment constituted anything more than tokenism was debatable, but at least there was a pretence of a supporter's voice in the important decisions.

Eddie Gray's promotion ambitions were unhinged by a disastrous opening run of five winless games, including an embarrassing 6-2 thrashing at Stoke. Leeds were stranded in the bottom three and there was hysteria in the boardroom.

A subsequent recovery saw Leeds find the safe haven of mid-table but the damage had been done. Gray was a popular man at Elland Road, loved by everybody; he had been part of the furniture for twenty-two years. However, the directors grumbled that nice guys rarely finished first and argued that more was needed. Strident voices asked whether Gray was strong enough to lead the team to promotion. The response was negative.

When the news leaked out the day before the home game with Middlesbrough in October, there were shockwaves around the city. Earlier in the week, things seemed to be on the up when two goals from Snodin inspired a League Cup victory at Walsall.

A local journalist rang Gray to ask about the team for the Boro game. Gray spilled the beans and the story spread like wildfire. Admitting that he 'had a feeling that this was coming', Gray took the news with dignity – when he met the players to bid farewell, he urged them to do their best for the club and behave like professionals.

Others did all Gray's talking for him.

The board was split 6-2 over the decision with Maxwell Holmes and Brian Woodward voting against the motion to remove Gray. Woodward, a former reserve team player and the son of former chairman Percy, resigned, saying, 'I may not go back to watch the team again and if I do, it certainly will not be in the directors' box.'

The players were even more set in their opposition, skipper Peter Lorimer reading out a prepared statement. 'We are amazed and astonished at the decision. The timing, immediately prior to a home match, is disturbing and unsettling, but far more important is our sympathy and concern for Eddie. He has worked selflessly for the last three years in the interests of the club and has built a team poised to enter the promotion stakes. The decision is absolutely demoralising.'

Two thousand fans staged a protest at the stadium, chanting, 'Silver out' and 'Bring back Eddie'. Earlier they had flooded the switchboard with protest calls and massed outside the main entrance. Directors and officials hurried inside past mounted policemen as the angry supporters waved a giant banner declaring, 'We want Eddie back.'

The chanting continued throughout the match, which Leeds won 1-0. Before the game Silver spoke to the players, as he revealed to the press after the game. 'They accepted my decision as professionals, although they did not agree with me … We will have a board meeting in midweek to discuss the managership. I must stress that nothing has changed. Eddie Gray is an extremely likeable man and I'm not surprised by the feelings of the fans.'

'We won this one for Eddie,' said a defiant Lorimer after the 1-0 victory, achieved via a penalty that the United captain had considered missing deliberately as a protest.

With the board adamant that there would be no change of heart, speculation quickly moved on to who would replace Gray. Names bandied about included former players – many favoured Jack Charlton or the Bradford City team of Trevor Cherry and Terry Yorath, even Lorimer. There was a bizarre suggestion that Tommy Docherty could be in the frame, but the hottest tip was for a 'dream ticket' of Don Revie and Johnny Giles returning to the club as a partnership with the Irishman as chief coach and Revie as general manager.

Speculation ran away with itself when it was reported that Giles had watched the Walsall game from the stands while Revie's initially positive comments added fuel to the fire. For a while, the suggestion seemed to make eminent sense but the story was stopped in its tracks when Revie insisted that he had no interest in the job. He told the media, 'What we did at Leeds was a bit special and you cannot turn the clock back. I do not want the Leeds job. To return to the club would be wrong at my time of life.'

A year earlier, Revie had been in the running for a return to football with QPR but fell out with Rangers chairman Jim Gregory over the package. The QPR supremo said, 'The terms he asked for then were not those he was seeking when I met him. In view of his increased demands, I have unfortunately come to the conclusion that I no longer wish Mr Revie to be the new manager of Queens Park Rangers.'

Revie ended up working part-time for Total Sport, the sports booking company run by his son Duncan, before retiring with his wife Elsie to Scotland.

It was another name from the past who eventually took on the poisoned chalice: the board recruited former captain Billy Bremner, championed by Revie, from Doncaster Rovers.

Bremner had left Leeds in 1976 to join Hull City and took on the Donny job in late 1978 when he was passed over for the manager's post at Boothferry Park. He could not prevent Doncaster finishing in the bottom three of the entire Football League, but after they successfully applied for re-election, Bremner led them to promotion from the Fourth Division in 1981. He struggled to maintain their status and two years later they were relegated.

His status as a Leeds legend went a long way to securing the job for Bremner, but it was said that what sealed the appointment was the way Bremner had played hardball when Leeds negotiated the purchase of Ian Snodin. That was a skill coveted by the directors given United's difficulties. The £45,000 paid in compensation to Doncaster to break Bremner's contract was felt to be a sound investment.

Bremner's first game, away to Barnsley on 27 October, brought a 3-0 defeat. He was furious and decided on immediate action. He had already stripped Lorimer of the captaincy, preferring the leadership of Snodin, and now he ruthlessly dispensed with the services of his former teammate, who left for non-league Whitby.

Bremner also consigned Gray's youth development programme to the bin, convinced that the only way to get out of the Second Division was with a mature squad. He dispensed with many of the young players that Gray had brought through the ranks, opting instead for older journeymen. It was a move that did not endear him to fans who had welcomed Gray's 'grow your own' policy.

Within months of Lorimer's exit, a host of young talent was shown the door. Out went Andy Linighan, Martin Dickinson, Terry Phelan, Denis Irwin, Scott Sellars and Tommy Wright. More prosaic players such as Brian Caswell, Ronnie Robinson, Bob Taylor, David Rennie, Brendon Ormsby,

John Buckley, Peter Haddock and Jack Ashurst were brought in to fill the void. Bremner did not throw all his toys out of the pram, relying on John Sheridan and Snodin as his midfield kingpins.

Bremner had a difficult start with just seven victories in his first twenty-four games, including an FA Cup exit at Fourth Division Peterborough. At the end of March, Leeds were fourth from bottom, staring down the barrel of a desperate fall into the Third Division.

Bremner somehow managed to coax enough out of his underperforming squad to save the day. From nowhere they delivered three straight victories in the first two weeks of April, sufficient for a safe passage. Bremner owed a significant debt to Andy Ritchie and his eight goals in as many games as Leeds finished fourteenth – the exact same position they had occupied when Gray was fired. It was a narrower squeak than it appeared; United finished just seven points clear of relegation and were in danger until the final fortnight. At their best, Leeds were a match for anyone in the division, but their best days came round far too rarely.

Bremner could trade on his legendary status for a while – gradually the fans came to accept his mantra that promotion required a revolution rather than the organic development advocated by his predecessor. But they looked back on the demise of Gray with genuine regret that he was not given the time to see the project through to its end.

CHAPTER EIGHT

Edge of Glory

After the fanfare when he took over, the rest of Billy Bremner's first season as United manager passed without any blinding flash, anything near the brilliance that he and the board had hoped for. He remained confident in his abilities, however, rallying the troops in the summer and declared that he would quit if he hadn't got Leeds promoted within two years.

Bremner spent the summer resisting Everton's dogged pursuit for Ian Snodin, with the clichéd insistence that he was not for sale at any price. It was a different tale as far as George McCluskey, Gary Hamson and Scott Sellars were concerned, although the club banked a paltry £20,000 from their departures. Bremner's refashioning of the squad continued apace as he added a couple of obscure midfielders in Russell Doig and John Buckley and signed Carlisle defender Jack Ashurst, the three costing £85,000 between them. There was a marquee signing, though, in Sheffield United goal-getter Keith Edwards, who had recently notched the 200th league goal of his career. Bremner considered the £125,000 a wise investment if Edwards could provide the cutting edge he needed.

A half-million loss had consumed much of the reserves built up by the sale of the stadium and fresh loans from Leslie Silver and the board were needed to fund Bremner's work in the market.

Bill Fotherby did what he could to help, negotiating a £50,000 shirt sponsorship deal with local clothiers the Burton Group. Peter Ridsdale, managing director of the chain, was a lifelong fan of Leeds United, and frequently to be seen in the club's executive restaurant. When Fotherby spotted him in there, he made a point of getting to know him. Fotherby was the most persuasive of characters and a starry-eyed Ridsdale was completely taken in, beguiled by talk of a future seat on the board. Fotherby had an eye for the main chance and wheedling the sponsorship money out of Ridsdale was relatively straightforward for such a savvy operator.

Bremner's rebuilding plans bore no immediate fruit – the team had a stumbling start with Edwards looking out of touch in the opener at Blackburn. Old faithful Andy Ritchie got on the scoresheet but Leeds recrossed the Pennines without a point after a 2-1 defeat.

Edwards' wait for a goal went on and on. It took six games for him to break his duck, his goal against Reading on 13 September helping Leeds to a 3-2 victory. Nevertheless, Bremner's new side had settled, and the three points took them fifth.

It was a false dawn for Edwards, who managed a miserly three goals in his first twenty-nine appearances. There were knowing nods from the terraces as another big name flopped at Elland Road. Too many examples over the years, they grumbled, the deep well of expectation drowning all but the most resilient.

The customary unruly behaviour of United fans had been happily absent for months but suddenly the old problems reignited. An improvement had been facilitated by an all-ticket restriction for away games, with the introduction of a membership scheme ensuring only supporters' club members, season ticketholders and shareholders could gain entrance.

Second Division chairmen had been quick to bellyache about the loss of income and campaigned for compensation. There was no way the FA would put their hands in their own pockets, so the only solution was to drop the ban. Lulled into a false sense of security, they promptly ditched the all-ticket order, allowing the thugs to return.

With the first game following the U-turn a high-profile local derby against Bradford City, the decision was high risk. It was also insensitive in the extreme; it was little more than a year since the dreadful fire at Valley Parade. Inevitably, fighting broke out inside the stadium and a fish and chip van got caught in the middle, overturned and set alight. The mid-1980s were a febrile breeding ground for such tribal warfare whenever rivals came to town. There was a twenty-minute delay in play while the ground was emptied and the game was played out to vacant stands, City winning 2-0.

Trouble spilled onto the streets surrounding the stadium, with unruly mobs of white, black and Asian youths rampaging down Manchester Road. Two policemen were attacked when they intervened – one suffered a broken leg and the other had to be given oxygen by paramedics. A youth from Leeds was stabbed in the stomach near the bus station and the area was left looking like a war zone. There were more than sixty arrests, including supporters from other clubs attracted by the likelihood of a ruck. Some of those taken into custody hailed from Blackburn and Ipswich.

The *Daily Star* made strident calls for Leeds United to be closed down. 'The louts of Leeds have got away with it for far too long. They have terrorised the terraces, tormented town centres and driven away many decent, honest followers of football. Too often they have been let off the hook. We are sick to the back teeth of the prattling succession of managers, directors and administrators who have told us "It's only a minority." That minority has been involved in thirteen savage incidents over the last forty months. Today, we regret to say, the authorities have only one course open to them. Leeds United must be closed down.'

A furious Leslie Silver fired back, reminding everyone that he had asked for the all-ticket rule to remain in place. After announcing that it would launch another investigation, the FA was only too happy to about face and reintroduce the restrictions. Now that the horse had bolted, the club introduced a red card identity system.

While the storm continued to rage in the media, the Leeds players quietly got on with business. They rose to second in October before three successive defeats over the next month saw them slip to sixth. They rallied again but faced a real smack in the face with an extraordinary 7-2 hammering at Stoke a few days before Christmas.

The *Yorkshire Evening Post* denounced the shoddy performance as 'miserably inadequate, spineless and embarrassing'. Bremner was forced into a change of tack and decided to cash in on Everton's dogged pursuit of Snodin. The fans protested vigorously at what they saw as a suicidal move but the £800,000 received, as well as setting a new club record, gave Bremner scope to rebuild. He might have lost his main man but a widespread strengthening of the squad revived a season that was threatening to implode. In came Coventry's Micky Adams and Oxford's Bobby McDonald along with Welsh international midfielder Mark Aizlewood and lanky striker John 'Big Bird' Pearson from Charlton. It was a huge gamble but there was a handsome pay-off with Leeds enjoying the most golden of springs.

Bremner immediately conferred the captaincy on Aizlewood, who freely acknowledged that it was the attraction of working with the Scot that persuaded him to forsake First Division football. Whatever the fans feared and logic suggested, Leeds were still a big draw with Bremner at the helm.

A post-Christmas revival included an unlikely assault on the FA Cup that began in less than auspicious circumstances away to non-league Telford United.

The David and Goliath nature of the pairing provoked immediate speculation as to what might happen when Leeds' notorious supporters descended on Telford's tiny Bucks Head stadium. A groundsman's hut had been set on fire during United's recent game at West Bromwich Albion, and it was clear that staging the cup tie in Telford was asking for trouble. The police decreed the risk too great and demanded that the match should be played at a venue better equipped to cope with trouble. There was a bizarre suggestion that the game could be staged at Elland Road, but that was quickly dismissed.

The game was switched to The Hawthorns in Birmingham with a Sunday lunchtime kick-off to dampen the chances of an alcohol-fuelled rampage.

The decision was roundly condemned as a victory for hooligans. The vast gap in status between the two clubs meant that the neutrals were already massed behind Telford – even the heavily pro-Leeds *Yorkshire Evening Post* openly rooted for Telford, trumpeting, 'For the first time in its history, the *YEP* today hopes Leeds United will lose a match.'

Bremner's efforts to shield the players from the animosity were effective and Ian Baird settled nerves with an early goal. But a bitterly cold day and a pitch made treacherous by ice were great levellers. Leeds were rocked on their heels as Telford got into their stride. Driven by adrenaline and the chance of making the headlines, they snatched a goal and threatened several more.

As the game settled, the odds moved heavily towards a replay until Baird came good again at the death, a ferocious long-range strike settling the outcome.

The fourth-round draw sent Leeds to Third Division Swindon, the fixture again scheduled for Sunday lunchtime. The weather was so bad that the game was called off on Sunday and rescheduled for Tuesday evening.

With touts openly flogging tickets outside the away part of the ground, a clutch of Swindon fans and others looking for a scrap found their way into the Leeds end and the game kicked off with some unsavoury scuffling on the terraces.

Swindon were a decent side in those days and on their way to a second successive promotion. Forcing Leeds onto the back foot, they got the early goal their football merited. The United players refused to panic and got back on terms when a Swindon defender put past his own keeper. Finding their form, they secured victory courtesy of another Baird goal.

United's reward was a home tie against First Division Queens Park Rangers.

Hordes of fans flocked to Elland Road for its biggest day in years. Gates were closed long before kick-off, the attendance of 31,324 the highest since February 1982. It was claimed that an error in Leeds' rudimentary computer system led to the official figure being understated. Certainly, there were thousands packing the area outside the stadium when the match began.

Urged on by the partisan crowd, Leeds took the battle to their opponents. The talismanic Baird was at it again, opening the scoring after eighteen minutes. He plunged full-length to head home after Pearson nodded an Adams centre back across goal.

Leeds continued to pin Rangers back with some enthusiastic football but a grim silence fell on the ground when David Rennie lucklessly conceded an own goal.

The setback only roused Leeds to greater efforts. QPR misread the runes, content to play for the draw. Their caution worked against them, inviting Leeds to kitchen sink attack.

With five minutes left and the fans raising the roof, Leeds threw everyone forward for a corner. The wall of noise seemed to inspire Brendon Ormsby as he came sailing in to billow the net with a wonderful header. The crowd massed behind the goal erupted as Ormsby ran towards them and leaped onto the fence to celebrate.

This was one of those moments when all the cares, woes and embarrassments of the previous decade could be forgotten. One of the most passionate sets of supporters in the country exploded with unreserved joy. What it was to be a Leeds fan that day!

The draw was kind to United and in the sixth round they faced Third Division Wigan Athletic, the lowest-placed team still in the cup. The tie was staged at humble Springfield Park, a stadium little changed from the Latics' days in the Northern Premier League. Its 12,000 capacity prompted the usual questions about whether the match should be relocated but the tie went ahead as planned with another Sunday lunchtime kick-off. The police set up roadblocks all around the tiny Lancashire town to guard against any invasion.

With Ormsby and Baird suspended and Aizlewood cup-tied, Leeds struggled to impose themselves as they played into the teeth of the gale that swept the quaint old stadium.

Wigan were clearly up for it – they had plenty of chances, the best of which was headed against the woodwork by Bobby Campbell – but Leeds retaliated strongly after the break, buoyed by the strong wind at their backs. From a corner, midfielder John Stiles fired Leeds ahead. Micky Adams made things safe late on and incredibly Leeds were into the last four for the first time in a decade.

They had plenty of time to get used to the idea, with four weeks between the sixth round and the semi-finals. Form was good in the meantime with Leeds bolstering their status in the promotion chase. The gap to the two automatic positions was a massive sixteen points but Leeds' chances were enhanced by the introduction of a new play-off system to help determine promotion.

Arrangements were slightly different in that first year. The Football League had agreed that the top flight should be reduced from twenty-two teams to twenty, with the other two added to the Second Division. To avoid too drastic a transition, in this first year the bottom three teams in Division One would be automatically relegated, but the side in nineteenth place would get a second chance, pitched in with three Second Division sides. The same would happen the following season before adopting the current situation where the teams finishing between third and sixth contest the play-offs.

The new opportunity gave Bremner every reason to hope for double glory at the end of an extraordinary season.

Those few shining weeks were a real anomaly in a dark decade for Leeds fans. The team rose above the dire amalgam of poor football, hooliganism and financial difficulties to show that there was an honest to goodness football club still alive and kicking. Hopes persisted that one day, some day, it might yet all come right.

The semi-final pitched Leeds against First Division Coventry with the game staged at Sheffield Wednesday's Hillsborough. It was a gorgeous day with the game beamed by delayed telecast to the nation by ITV. The previous day at Villa Park, Tottenham hammered Watford 4-1 in the other game, the boring one.

Coventry were comfortable in the upper reaches of Division One at the time, undergoing a renaissance under the management of John Sillett. They had giants in goal and at the centre of defence in Steve Ogrizovic and Brian Kilcline; further forward they offered genuine threat with winger Dave Bennett providing the ammunition for Cyrille Regis, always a thorn in Leeds' side during his days at West Brom.

Few people gave Leeds a hope but it was they who had the better start, on the front foot and in Coventry faces from the off. They reaped the reward for their ambition after seventeen minutes when David Rennie headed them into a shock lead.

Confidence high, Leeds bossed the game for the first hour. Then the tide turned.

Ormsby seemed to have things under control as he shepherded a Coventry forward ball towards the goal line, but he misjudged the moment and Bennett came away with the ball. Micky Gynn, who had just come on for Coventry, slammed home Bennett's centre with relish.

Defeat seemed inevitable when Keith Houchen gave City the lead with ten minutes remaining, but back came Leeds with Keith Edwards heading an equaliser in the finest moment of his Leeds career. The goal sparked wild celebrations from the players and the terraces swayed with gleeful abandon.

The adrenaline of the moment gave Leeds fresh heart, but legs had gone and the lottery of extra-time was too much for the United players. They had run themselves into the ground and were forced to admit defeat when Bennett forced a winner.

'This should have been the final' was the comment at the end of one of the best semi-finals in years.

Being part of someone else's history was no consolation to Leeds, but they still had the hope of promotion and there was no post-match collapse. Five wins out of the final eight games were enough to deliver fourth place and qualification for the play-offs.

For First Division Charlton Athletic the arrangements offered a last-chance saloon. A 2-1 win against QPR on the final day saw them take the crucial nineteenth position at the expense of Leicester. They seized the opportunity, seeing off Ipswich, who had finished fifth in Division Two, to qualify for the two-legged play-off final.

The first leg of Leeds' pairing with third-placed Oldham 'was a match that had plenty of passion but little football', according to *The Times*' Martin Searby. The game, delayed by fifteen minutes due to the congestion caused by a crowd of 29,472, was played out in a frenetic atmosphere. Oldham looked to have survived the Leeds bombardment until substitute Keith Edwards popped up with a vital winner in the eighty-ninth minute.

With the second leg to be played on the plastic pitch at Boundary Park, Leeds' late goal was priceless. The return match was a Sunday high noon affair and 5,000 United fans swelled the crowd to a season's best of 19,216. The presence of former United trio Denis Irwin, Andy Linighan and Tommy Wright in the Oldham line-up brought added spice to the game.

Athletic seemed to have the advantage when Gary Williams levelled the tie after eighteen minutes, and with just ninety seconds remaining, Mike Cecere headed in an Irwin cross to send the Oldham players and fans into raptures. Leeds were not yet dead and super sub Edwards had a say again, scoring while Oldham celebrations were still dying down.

The wind had gone from the Oldham sails as the match tumbled into extra-time. With no further scores, the away goal sent Leeds through to a final against Charlton.

'We finished seven points clear of Leeds, so to go out on away goals to them means there is something unjust,' bemoaned Oldham boss Joe Royle. 'I welcomed the play-offs but possibly hadn't considered the long-term ramifications.'

There was no grand one-off final at Wembley in those days and the two teams played out a low-key final over two legs.

Leeds went into the games in confident mood, despite the supposed superiority of the First Division Addicks. There was little between the two teams, though Charlton edged the first game at Selhurst Park 1-0. The goal came late from Jim Melrose.

With John Pearson injured a few days before the second leg, Bremner was forced to call twenty-year-old striker Bob Taylor back from holiday to replace him.

In a fearsome encounter played out in front of Leeds' best crowd of the season (31,395), the second leg threatened to boil over, the enormity of what was at stake too much for some. Charlton were in determined mood and it was a tense and bruising evening with tackles flying in and tempers frayed.

In between the confrontations, Leeds carved out the best chance of the game, with McDonald's centre finding Sheridan after Baird and keeper Bob Bolder disputed possession. Sheridan landed the ball on the crossbar and Taylor could not reach the rebound.

Leeds fans were afforded the moment they craved after fifty-four minutes. When Aizlewood's shot cannoned off a Charlton defender, Taylor seized on the loose ball. Peter Shirtliff's tackle sent him tumbling, but the ball was already travelling towards goal and Ormsby popped up to make doubly sure to level the tie and spark an explosion of joy.

Leeds poured forward in their quest for a killer second, and it took a last-ditch header from Shirtliff to save Charlton with Baird preparing to pounce. Leeds sent on Edwards in search of a late winner, but he had no trick in his box this time.

Of a bruising encounter, Shirtliff commented, 'It's not football, it's a boxing match. There's no enjoyment whatsoever in these matches. People are just charging about crashing into each other because of what's at stake. They have both been bruising battles.'

The deadlock caught the FA unprepared and an unanticipated replay was arranged for Birmingham's St Andrew's four days later.

Intervention from the authorities saw the match limited to 18,000 spectators. Three-hundred police were on duty for the Friday evening kick-off as an estimated 16,000 Leeds fans descended upon Birmingham. United supporters had queued overnight to obtain tickets and packed the Spion Kop terrace, the Railway End, most of the main stand ... everywhere, while 3,000 Londoners were tucked away in one corner.

The pattern of the game was as edgy and irritable as the previous encounters, with tackles flying in on all sides. Skipper Ormsby was forced to limp off after he came out second best from a fierce tackle on Garth Crooks.

There was little in the way of excitement and after a dull ninety minutes, the game went into extra-time with the prospect of penalties looming large. That would have been no way to settle such a contest and after ten minutes Leeds seemed to have put things to rest.

Stiles' long through ball was headed down by Pearson for Edwards to drive goalwards. Paul Miller was judged to have handled and Leeds were awarded a free kick 30 yards out. Up stepped the maestro, John Sheridan. He paced out his run and coolly clipped the ball over the wall and beyond the reach of goalkeeper Bolder – the First Division beckoned Leeds as the ball found the net.

It was one of those moments in the colourful history of Leeds United, on the brink of glory as the crowd went wild. St Andrew's was a sea of bleary-eyed glee as Sheridan threw his hands to his head in unrestrained joy. We're going up!

But Fate was not kind to Leeds that night. Everything fell apart in the second period of extra-time as Shirtliff scored twice. Everyone connected with Leeds was in bits, their elation of minutes earlier replaced by despair.

The emotion-soaked fans refused to leave the scene until the players came back out to acknowledge them. Thirteen minutes went by before Bremner and his men had recovered enough to join the travelling thousands in a sad sharing of 'might have beens'. It was an empty and dispirited journey home for fans and players after an evening of massive highs and plunging lows.

The pain took an age to dissipate but when it had, spirits began to rise, boosted by the knowledge that finally United were back and could hope again for a brighter future.

'It's been a great season for us despite this final blow and we can now use our experience as a springboard for next season,' reflected Leslie Silver. 'I am sure we will be there again.'

CHAPTER NINE

Why Would Maradona Want to Come *Here*?

Bill Fotherby prided himself on his ability to drum up cash.

'We always knew where the money was,' he said. 'People thought we'd won the pools ... I could always go to a sponsor and say, "Look, we want to sign Gary McAllister, can you let me have £200,000 from next season's sponsorship? Please let me have it because he will make the difference," and invariably I would get the money that I wanted.'

Fotherby was also a master publicist, his flair for grabbing the headlines never better demonstrated than during one infamous episode in the autumn of 1987. There was nothing more to it than a flight of fancy in Fotherby's mind and a few words in the right ears, but he had Fleet Street eating out of the palm of his hand for weeks.

'Maradona to meet Bremner?' pondered one local paper over a claim that Leeds had made 'a sensational £10 million bid to get Diego Maradona'. It whispered conspiratorially of 'a business consortium ... set up to raise the money and bring about the most amazing transfer deal in British football'.

'Talks have already taken place between United, their main sponsors, Burton, and Maradona's English agent, Jon Smith,' went the story put about by Fotherby, 'and hopes are still high that the Argentinian captain will leave Naples in Italy for Leeds.'

If only someone had told Burton's Peter Ridsdale, then he might have been in a better place to respond to questions from his bosses and the media. Instead, he blankly opened and closed his mouth in astonishment. Not for the last time would the words 'goldfish' and 'Ridsdale' appear in the same sentence.

Maradona was the biggest name in world football at the time, a year on from inspiring his country to a World Cup triumph with the despicable 'Hand of God' goal in the quarter-final against England.

It was all bunkum, of course, a pack of lies dreamed up by Fotherby to generate column inches for Leeds United, and he was bullish when Ridsdale tackled him about the matter.

'You never know where such speculation might lead to ... Look, Peter, all I said was that we had been in discussion with his agent. *True*. Because we were. And that you were present. *True*. Because you were. I really can't help what the press make of that...'

Burton were apoplectic about the affair but Ridsdale really couldn't help being rather amused (with hindsight) by Fotherby's cheek. The story certainly kept Leeds on the front pages.

Fotherby's actions had completely blindsided Billy Bremner, who was kept in the dark throughout, and it was anybody's guess as to how the South American could have been accommodated in a Leeds team. Bremner showed the greatest restraint, however, toeing the party line while there was a chance of the coup coming off.

The stories served to distract supporters from the summer sale of Ian Baird and that might have been part of the plan. The striker, a real cult hero, was off for a shot at the First Division with promoted Portsmouth in a £285,000 deal. Andy Ritchie was also gone, swelling the growing ranks of former Leeds players at Oldham, while Keith Edwards ended his Elland Road nightmare with a move to Aberdeen. While Edwards had been a failure and would not be missed, United fans were apprehensive about the team's goal-scoring capabilities. It was anybody's guess where the goals would come from. A pairing of Big Bird Pearson and twenty-year-old Bob Taylor was not the most inspiring of partnerships.

Bremner's only purchases of note were two overpriced defenders, Ian Snodin's brother Glynn leaving Sheffield Wednesday for a £150,000 fee and Aston Villa full-back Gary Williams signed in a £230,000 deal. Jim Melrose, who had scored for Charlton in the play-offs against Leeds, arrived in a low-key £50,000 deal, but was gone a few months later, sold to Shrewsbury after failing to score in the six games he managed.

'Not good enough,' muttered the fans. 'And why on earth would Maradona ever want to come *here*?' Their worst fears were borne out – United had an appalling start to the season, with just two narrow victories and three goals from the first nine games, two of them from Sheridan. Toiling in sixteenth place, it was all too depressing after such an extraordinary season had led bookies to install Leeds as favourites for promotion.

Bremner's initial response to the lack of goals was to take a lesson from the past, asking reserve defender Peter Swan to try his luck up front. There was to be no John Charles-like conversion – Swan scored three times in his first four games, but it was obvious that he was no long-term solution. Bremner recognised as much, persuading Leslie Silver and the board to allow the bank overdraft to drift northwards to free up £350,000 for the recruitment of Derby striker Bobby Davison.

The twenty-eight-year-old was a decent punt. He had earned a good reputation, scoring 112 goals in 271 games for Huddersfield, Halifax and Derby.

Davison enjoyed a scoring debut against Swindon on 21 November, though there were only 15,457 souls on hand to observe the 4-2 victory. David Rennie set things in motion after two minutes with an opening goal from close range following a corner and Davison made it 2-0 before the half-hour, slamming home when Swindon failed to clear. Bob Taylor added a third before the break, but United allowed the Wiltshire side back into the game in the second period.

Bobby Barnes snatched a brace and had another goal chalked off for offside – Leeds' one-goal advantage looked shaky with thirteen minutes to see out, sparking groans around the barren stadium.

Six minutes from time, though, Peter Haddock became an unlikely saviour. The defender shocked everybody when he ventured into the rarefied atmosphere of the attacking third, played a one-two with John Stiles on the edge of the Swindon area, tiptoed through the defence and poked home the fourth goal in fine style. It was his first and last goal for Leeds.

Among the Swindon ranks that day were thirty-year-old David Hockaday, a shock choice as Leeds manager some twenty-seven years later, and future Blackburn and England keeper Tim Flowers.

Davison was not the only Leeds debutant – the crowd were getting their first sight of a tigerish young midfielder. The player in question was David Batty, gifted an opportunity by John Sheridan's suspension. Eleven days before his nineteenth birthday, Batty enjoyed a fine debut, showcasing his neat short passing and biting tackles. He came close to a goal himself, played through but blazing his shot narrowly wide. In later years, he would become a Leeds legend in a holding midfield role but against Swindon he seemed only too happy to shoot on sight, popping up in dangerous positions on several occasions.

Batty quickly made himself an automatic choice in the middle of the park, missing just two of United's final twenty-five league games. It was obvious what Bremner saw in him, a mirror image of himself with his fierce challenges, jutted-out chin and lack of respect for opponents. Before the end of the season, he had made his debut for England Under-21s – Bremner had unearthed a real diamond in the rough.

Just as a callow newcomer was about to establish himself, the club bade farewell to one of its old-timers – on 5 October, vice-chairman Manny Cussins passed away, three weeks short of his eighty-second birthday. He had served twenty-six years on the board, eleven of them as chairman.

Cussins' seat at the boardroom table had been taken two weeks earlier by Peter Ridsdale, managing director at Topman. Hearing that QPR were courting Ridsdale with the promise of a directorship, Bill Fotherby secured him a spot on the condition that Burton's sponsorship of Leeds continued. Aged just thirty-five, Ridsdale became United's youngest director.

The introduction of Davison gave Leeds fresh bite up front and sparked an upturn in form. They enjoyed a decent December, five straight league victories lifting them into the top half of the table. The improvement prompted a massive hike in attendances. The 36,004 who watched Leeds beat Bradford City on New Year's Day was the highest in the league since April 1981. The improved attendances made a massive difference to the club's finances, though the heavy outlay in the transfer market turned a trading profit into a bottom-line deficit.

That was the summit of their season. Even the cut-price £120,000 return of Ian Baird from Portsmouth could not do the trick, though he managed three goals in his first eight games. There were two notable victories – 4-1 against West Brom and 5-0 against Sheffield United with each game featuring a highly improbable contribution from John Pearson.

Big Bird's first forty-four appearances for Leeds had brought him just four goals, and it was he who made way when Davison arrived. Despite not making the bench for weeks, Pearson rejected a move to Shrewsbury in November, determined to fight for his place. Recalled by Bremner at the end of January after three successive defeats, Pearson repaid the show of faith by scoring in the defeat of West Brom. Two further goals in his next three games suddenly made Pearson flavour of the month.

Leeds' upward momentum brought an unlikely victory away to table-topping Aston Villa on 12 March and the following week's clash with Sheffield United came with Leeds' promotion chances looking good – they went into the game just four points shy of the fifth-place position that would provide entry to the play-offs. The afternoon was the finest in a Leeds shirt for the ungainly Pearson, a lifelong fan of the Blades' Sheffield rivals, Wednesday, for whom he racked up more than 100 appearances.

Heavy rain throughout the previous day had ruined a pitch which was already devoid of grass down the middle, showing the effects and the marking from its rugby league commitments. Morning sun had given way to drizzle, which continued throughout the afternoon, leaving the pitch in a bog-like state, suiting Pearson to a T.

Sheffield were tottering towards relegation and fell behind when Swan, now restored to his customary role in the back four, opened the scoring after eighty seconds. The Blades made it to the break with no further concessions but were shaken by the loss of midfielder Wally Downes as the clock ran down. Downes had recklessly thrust an elbow into the face of Mark

Aizlewood as the two contested an aerial ball in the Leeds area. He was shown a yellow for that one and got his marching orders a few minutes later after illegally hampering a Leeds breakaway.

Sheridan came on at half-time for a dazed Aizlewood and promptly began to run the game. He opened the way for the second goal eight minutes after the resumption by setting up Gary Williams on the right wing. Pearson nodded in from the full-back's well-placed cross. Minutes later, Sheridan put Leeds three ahead when the ball ran out to him from a poor Sheffield clearance. He clipped a smart drive inside the right post, giving the keeper no chance.

As the game entered its final ten minutes, Pearson netted twice within the space of sixty seconds. The first saw him almost face down on the 6-yard line as he threw himself full-length to nod home a low cross and then he poked in from about a yard out after Ian Baird carved his way through on the left byline. Pearson wasn't quite sure what to do with himself as the bemused crowd celebrated. The mud which caked him head to toe made the white of his kit almost invisible.

Leeds' advance was stymied by a run of four games without a victory but they remained in contention for the play-offs until 23 April, when a failure to beat Oldham at Elland Road coupled with Aston Villa's victory against Shrewsbury condemned them to a seventh season in the Second Division.

The fans had seen it all before, of course. They knew far better than to expect success but they could console themselves with the form of Sheridan. The Manchester-born schemer shone through all United's best moments – he top scored with twelve goals, seven of them from the penalty spot. It was enough to earn him a first full cap for Ireland in March 1988 when he helped them beat Romania 2-0.

CHAPTER TEN

Marching Altogether

After the golden promise of the previous twelve months, the 1987/88 season saw the hopes of supporters ground into the dust yet again. The standard Leeds United follower is a curious amalgam of self-flagellation and dry gallows humour, but he approaches every season with rose-tinted spectacles firmly attached to his nose. There was no difference in the summer of 1988 – fans hoped against hope that this would be the year as Leeds were once again installed as promotion favourites. Supporter loyalty was evidenced by the £500,000 raised in season ticket sales.

Billy Bremner was as optimistic as any fan but recognised that his squad required strengthening. He cut away some dead wood, dispensing with the services of Nigel Thompson, Jim Melrose, Russell Doig, Ken De Mange and Bobby McDonald for a total sum of £140,000 and set out to exploit Portsmouth's relegation from the First Division by snapping up some bargains. He had already brought Ian Baird back from Fratton Park in March, the £120,000 a pittance for a player whom he had sold for £285,000 less than twelve months earlier. Now he brought in burly Jamaica-born centre-back Noel Blake on a free transfer and then added former Crystal Palace, England B and Under-21 winger Vince Hilaire. Pompey wanted £270,000 but a tribunal set a final fee of £170,000 and Bremner pronounced himself well satisfied.

In retrospect, the recruitment of two black footballers into a club that attracted a fair few racist followers seemed to be a risky strategy. An unhealthy seam of racism still ate away at the heart of Leeds – little had changed since the appalling case of David Oluwale, a British Nigerian, 'hounded to his death' by police in the city in 1969. His death led to the first prosecution of British police for involvement in the death of a black person.

Blake, affectionately dubbed 'Bruno' by the fans, recalled,

I played at Elland Road on a few occasions but it was in the 1985/86 season that I remember the visit for the wrong reasons. Leeds won the game 2-1 with two Lyndon Simmonds goals but I received some terrible abuse from a section of the Leeds fans.

As a kid I had followed Leeds, they were my second team behind Birmingham City and the treatment I got that day hurt me, although I must admit, I had to put up with racist chants most weeks and that's how it was back then.

When the opportunity came to sign for Billy Bremner, God bless him, it was one I couldn't refuse. I asked myself, 'Do you shy away or do you face the challenge?' I faced the challenge and signed for the club and it was a real pleasure to play for Leeds United. I never had a single problem with the supporters during my time there, they were superb with me.

Vince Hilaire also joined that summer and we went out into the community, educated people, broke down the barriers and laid some strong foundations and that was something I am extremely proud of.

Typically, Blake decided to tackle matters head on when he signed for the club.

'A journalist tried to collar me for some post-match quotes when I was walking out of the dressing room,' said Blake. 'He was running down this corridor and shouting, "Vince, Vince". Clearly, he thought I was Vince Hilaire. So I carried on and eventually he caught up with me, pulled my arm and said, "Vince?" I just looked at him and replied, "Sorry, wrong n****r, man," and walked off.

'Society has changed. But unless you're on the receiving end, you will never understand it. Politicians don't know what it's like.'

Bremner, Leslie Silver and the other directors had done what they could to drive the racists away and their cause was aided by West Yorkshire Police's infamous 'Wild Boar' operation. This was a covert police operation designed to address the chronic hooliganism that surrounded football. It sought to take down the ringleaders but led only to the conviction of a small number of minor players. Four police officers infiltrated the notorious Service Crew in one of the first and most successful of a series of undercover investigations into English hooligan gangs. It began around October 1986 and culminated in raids at more than a dozen addresses the following March. Those arrested, aged between seventeen and thirty, were charged with conspiracy to commit affray and later faced a six-week trial.

Ex-Para David Brown, who saw action in the Falklands War and was later diagnosed with post-traumatic stress disorder, was one of those involved and was given a four-year prison sentence.

'I'd supported Leeds all the way through the Paras and when I got out the in thing at the time were football firms. I'd got used to having drinking sessions with close mates in the army and this was what these lads offered me. We'd fight with other firms outside the grounds. But I started going through phases of just hitting people without even realising it. Even some of the lads were getting concerned.'

This uncontrolled violence was a symptom of Brown's illness but saw him arrested four times in 1985 and 1986 for football-related violence. In April 1987, he found himself in Leeds Crown Court along with a number of other suspected hooligans. The national press vilified him, branding him 'The General', and accused him of orchestrating the violence. He was found guilty on a charge of organised conspiracy to cause violence and jailed for four years, despite a plea from his defence to take into account the terrible effect of his experiences during the war.

Amidst this climate of hatred and prejudice, Blake and Hilaire were statement signings for Leeds United, leaving the fans in no doubt that 'we are a multi-cultural club'. Racism would not be tolerated. At the time, the face of Leeds United was almost entirely white, with one having to go back almost a decade to find the last black player to have an impact at Elland Road, Terry Connor, his acceptability enhanced by his local birth. A decade prior to Connor, the South African winger Albert Johanneson had been one of the most exciting wingers in English football until he was discarded by Don Revie, denounced as a coward and a drunk.

One of the most important drivers for change came with a fan-led initiative which had begun to gain traction a year earlier. It was launched by supporters who were weary of the racist atmosphere at Elland Road on a Saturday. They came together as Leeds Fans United against Racism and Fascism (LFUARAF), with the stated intention being 'to decisively change the culture at Elland Road through overtly challenging both racist behaviour amongst fans and the ongoing fascist political agitation in and around the ground'. Initial steps included the distribution of anti-racist stickers, leaflets and fixture calendars, and they subsequently launched the anti-racist fanzine *Marching Altogether*.

When asked why they started the campaign, one of the men behind LFUARAF commented,

The atmosphere at Elland Road was intolerable in 1987, both the racism in the ground and the fascists peddling their filth outside. The club said that there wasn't a problem ... We didn't get any support for our campaign. We had to do all the running ourselves.

We started with a couple of leaflets to test the water and lots of anti-fascists came to help us in that first year. The response was pretty mixed and we realised that the problem was that people felt outsiders were coming in to leaflet. What we needed was a campaign run by football fans themselves and the fanzine was the best way for us to do this. It gave us a chance to get our people listening to our ideas. We slagged off the fascists but we also talked about issues that affected the fans – all-seater stadia, the club treating fans badly, etc. The political message in the fanzine was strong but it wasn't all about well-intentioned lefties telling people what to think. It was about people that cared passionately about football and Leeds United and wanted to give people the confidence to speak up.

We used cartoons about fascists and football (nominating 'crap haircut' awards being our favourite). 'Dickhead in the crowd' was a way of pinpointing individual racists to shut them up.

It's worked because we've done more than just a campaign about racism. We hope we've made people think about these issues and we've tried to help change the atmosphere down there. The club's improved performance and the signing of black players has probably done much to change things.

Paradoxically, in its early days, it was LFUARAF who came under pressure from an establishment unwilling to recognise the depth of the problem. When the group gave West Yorkshire Police notice that they would be handing out leaflets in a peaceful and organised manner at a future match, the police, Leeds United and local media all tried to dissuade them, worrying that it would exacerbate the situation.

Superintendent Jack Clapham, the officer responsible for matchday policing at Elland Road, commented, 'My worry would be that the actions of this group will provoke a reaction from the National Front. It could prove a busy day for us when we are keeping rival fans apart.'

Leeds United also feared the worst, with club secretary David Dowse saying that he had no idea who was behind the leaflet and threatening legal action if the group used the club badge on its leaflets. They also refused to meet to discuss the issue, only agreeing after considerable political pressure from a local MP.

The club questioned LFUARAF's analysis of the problem and challenged them to produce evidence, thinking they would back down. Not a bit of it; LFUARAF responded instantly, publishing *Terror on our Terraces* in March 1988. It received significant national coverage with the *Daily Mirror* headlining with 'Fascist, racist and violent – club branded a breeding ground for the NF thugs'.

Wisely, the board realised the futility of swimming against the tide and took up the cudgels. Anti-racist leaflets signed by Billy Bremner and the players were distributed to fans at the turnstiles. It was a watershed moment for the club.

'Leslie Silver took over as chairman and that's when they asserted themselves,' recalled a LFUARAF representative. 'Silver was a really good bloke. We met him in later years and he was very supportive. I think the club just thought, "We need to get our act together on that." But we did have to force them.'

The presence of council members on the club board strengthened LFUARAF's hand. The group met with key councillors from the Labour-controlled Leeds City Council and demanded that action should be taken against racism in the ground. Similarly, the Police Commander was 'moved on to other duties' and replaced by a new commander with a more progressive attitude. He quickly began to hold constructive meetings with the campaign and, inevitably, the new approach was translated into a more enlightened attitude by police in their matchday duties.

The changes were not immediate, and hooliganism continued to haunt the club for some time, but a clear line had been drawn in the sand.

The recruitment of Blake and Hilaire forced supporters to reconsider their tolerance for the racist contingent among them. But while change was in the air in that respect, there was nothing new in terms of playing fortunes as Leeds stumbled through the opening month.

Given the presence of the three ex-Pompey players, it was ironic that United's first away game should take them to Portsmouth. A week earlier, the season had started with a disappointing 1-1 draw against Oxford. Things got worse on the south coast with Pompey handing out a 4-0 hiding and Baird sent off.

There was only one victory from the first six league games as Leeds slithered towards the bottom of the table and media speculation was rife that Bremner was about to carry the can. The day after a League Cup victory against Peterborough on 27 September, the board sacked the manager and put coach Peter Gunby in temporary charge.

Leslie Silver took the decision with a heavy heart, but it was obvious that something very different was needed. The spring of 1987 had been nothing more than a glorious anomaly – Leeds had not advanced under Bremner and were in much the same position as they were when Silver sacked Eddie Gray.

As the chairman said,

We had a meeting on Monday afternoon, we reviewed the situation as of the second half of last season, we looked at the situation that was emerging this season and we felt that it wasn't going to happen. And therefore as a board we had to make a decision. It was a hard one, but we felt that if we were going to have to bring someone new in at some time then the sooner the better. The situation is obviously as bad as it could be at the moment. We've had the odd win in six games. We thought it was the time to do it ... We look at the situation of a season as a whole.

The season before last we had a very good season with Billy Bremner but we didn't make the First Division. This city demands First Division football. We had 26,000 people, the second largest gate in the country, at Elland Road on Saturday, and we lost at home to Chelsea, it was a poor result, but that wasn't the factor, the factor was the overall pattern of play, the overall style of the football, the way things have gone on these last 12 months. We feel that Billy's tried hard, he's been a very good manager, I've worked well with him on a personal basis, but it hasn't worked, and therefore it's better to change.

Bremner, like Allan Clarke and Eddie Gray before him, was distraught at being unable to bring the success to Leeds he had experienced as a player but he kept his counsel, uttering not a word of criticism against the club or the board. Side before self every time!

As the board ditched its seventh manager since the departure of Don Revie, Leeds United were once again left to ponder on an uncertain future.

CHAPTER ELEVEN

Wilko

When the news came through of Billy Bremner's sacking all the usual suspects were trotted out as potential successors.

Leslie Silver and Bill Fotherby travelled to Spain to persuade Athletic Bilbao and former Everton manager Howard Kendall to take the job, but when those discussions proved fruitless, they turned their attention to a quarry closer to home. Taking up the recommendation of England manager Bobby Robson, who had himself been an initial target, and responding to the nagging of board member Jack Marjason, the directors sought out Sheffield Wednesday's Howard Wilkinson.

Few people, even among those on the board, really believed that Wilkinson, a coach on a steep upward trajectory, could be enticed to cross Yorkshire. After inspiring Notts County to an overperforming spell in the First Division in the early 1980s and coaching the England non-league side, he had transformed Wednesday into the county's most prominent club, one that threatened to embed itself in the upper echelons of the top tier.

'At the time, I was in the First Division with Sheffield Wednesday, so Bill and Leslie both said to Bobby Robson, "why would he come here?"' said Wilkinson. 'He just said "If you don't ask, you will never know."'

'They did ask and, if I remember rightly, I was talking to them for about two-and-a-half weeks. It didn't happen overnight because I wanted to know what their ambitions for the future were and where they wanted to go.'

'What I went [to Sheffield Wednesday] to do, I did in my first year, in a sense. The hard work starts then, though, because you are trying to stay in that top flight and better still, trying to get into the top six. We did qualify for Europe, but it was the year Heysel happened and English clubs were banned. Sheffield Wednesday had been in the top flight for a few years and I knew that we needed investment on the pitch to take the next step. If you don't do that, you go backwards and it wasn't available. I don't hold anything against them or the people there at that time, that was just the reality. Leeds came along, second bottom of the division below and once again, after I had spoken to then Leeds chairman Leslie Silver at length on a number of occasions, I felt that it was an opportunity to do what I wanted to do. I wanted to win the First Division, get into Europe and compete with the best.

'I had enjoyed my years at Hillsborough but I started to realise we had probably gone as far as we could. The previous summer, we had held a board meeting and it was clear the policy of investment would not change dramatically. My thinking was the club would only stagnate with that policy and I didn't want that.'

Wilkinson fully appreciated the depth of the challenge facing him at Leeds, saying later, 'Desolate … Desolate … Didn't own the ground, didn't have a decent training ground, second bottom of the league, in debt, not a lot of money, but all I saw was the opportunity, the opportunity to manage a club that I thought could genuinely compete in the then First Division … Having got to know Leslie Silver as well as I had and got to know how he felt and got him to understand what it was I wanted to do and the vision I had of where I wanted us to go, I was just very, very confident that despite the problems we could do what we set out to do.'

Wilkinson told the board there was a slow way of reviving Leeds and a quick way, before outlining a plan that involved promotion the following season and the league title 'within five or six years … I said the difference was about £2 million, which I knew from a look at the finances would have to be Leslie's money.'

Recognising that Leeds United was a club living in the past, trading on the memories of the Don Revie years, Wilkinson ordered that the stadium be stripped of the photos celebrating that golden past. He told people, 'When we are nearly or as good as them, then they can go back up.'

Wilkinson quickly got to work, transforming virtually everything including attitude, diet and match preparations. He also identified a need to root out a negative element in the squad and the importance of bringing in men who could show the way.

'There are always leaders who create the energy in a football club. The followers then feed off the leaders' energy. But then there might also be terrorists within the club. They drain energy. These terrorists also like company. Misery loves company.'

Wilkinson was universally and unfairly painted as dour. His wit was as dry as the Sahara and you only properly understood him when you were allowed through his aloof veneer. He was widely dismissed as a disciple of the long-ball game – certainly his teams played direct football and relied heavily on second phase plays. It was a calculated approach, playing the percentages, relying on getting the ball into areas where the opposition could be hurt and then following in rapidly. But Wilkinson's teams were packed with skilled and intelligent midfield players who could dominate the centre of the pitch. They were also intensively coached and drilled so things came as second nature for them. He would add flair when he had got Leeds out of the Second Division, but his team could play football and often did, to good effect.

This was a club, thought Wilkinson, that had the potential to rise to the top of the English game, to recover its former status, and everything about the project had to be exactly right. Nothing must be left to chance.

He was very clear about off-field matters, criticising some of the board's bureaucratic leanings and vagueness, and insisting that they had to go even further to eradicate the hooliganism and racism.

Ces Podd, the former Bradford City defender, was brought in as community relations manager, with the remit of improving the club's public image. Podd had carried out a similar job at Valley Parade and was an energetic force for change with United, with many of the players becoming advocates for a programme that repaired the club's tarnished reputation.

All of this set the scene and foundation for the modernisation of Leeds United, for the ditching of the baggage that had dogged the club for more than a decade.

For Wilkinson to earn the time for his grand plan to take effect, it was imperative that he rescued a season that was sliding towards disaster. Leeds were rooted in the bottom four and there was no time to lose. Wilkinson had an instant galvanising impact, quickly stabilising results with a single defeat from his first eleven games in charge. A 4-0 defeat of Stoke on 26 November took Leeds up to fourteenth and comparative safety.

There were a few defeats along the way, but Wilkinson had brought new spirit and resilience. He began to reshape the squad; his first imports in November were decidedly low-key – Witton Albion defender Mike Whitlow and Rotherham midfielder Andy Williams – but with the threat of relegation almost gone, he showed his true colours in March with the signings of Chris Fairclough and Gordon Strachan.

Fairclough was a neat and tidy centre-back at Tottenham but had lost his way since a move from Nottingham Forest. Wilkinson recognised his potential and splashed out £500,000 to bring him in.

It was Strachan, however, who was the key signing, the game-changer, just as Bobby Collins and Johnny Giles had been for Don Revie in the 1960s.

The diminutive thirty-two-year-old Scot had fallen out with Manchester United manager Alex Ferguson and declared surplus to requirements. He seemed set for a reunion with former Red Devils boss Ron Atkinson, who had taken over at Sheffield Wednesday, but Wilkinson worked his magic.

Somehow, I got hold of him: 'Do not go home from Sheffield, Gordon. Come to Elland Road first. We can give you a new career.' I told him

I was looking for someone who was more than a player. Someone who could be my conduit on the pitch. Someone who could support the culture I wanted to grow, and demonstrate it by the way he trains, talks, thinks and behaves. Someone to be club captain. I said we could get him fitter, prolong a career he thought was ending. I was delighted when he said yes.

When we met, I almost got the sense Gordon thought he had one foot in the deckchair. I made it clear that was not what I wanted. What I needed was someone who would be my leader on the pitch and the person I wanted everyone else to be. I knew that person didn't exist at the club.

Gordon signed and the rest, as they say, is history.

Leeds briefly hinted that they might qualify for the end-of-season play-offs, but fell away when the opportunity presented itself, finishing tenth. Going up had not been part of Wilkinson's game plan – promotion could wait, he needed to get the foundations right first, to ready things for a proper shot in his first full season.

One man who would not be part of that proper shot was Mark Aizlewood. The Welshman had retained the captaincy, even though it was evident that Wilkinson did not see him as part of his long-term plans. A transfer to Portsmouth was offered but Aizlewood did not fancy the move.

What did for him was a spat with the fans. Aizlewood had become a target for discontent among supporters and the heckling was both sustained and pointed – try as he might he could not get the crowd onside.

The end came in the May Day fixture against Walsall.

'I sensed that things were going to come to a head,' recalled Aizlewood.

My wife and daughter always came to the home games but I asked them to stay away that day. It was a typically dour end-of-season affair which was heading for a 0-0 draw and every time I touched the ball, the boos would ring out. With less than ten minutes remaining, Peter Haddock put a cross over and I managed to head it past the keeper. The Kop started celebrating and cheering. The same fans had been booing me for weeks and had slaughtered me all afternoon. My first thought was 'what a bunch of hypocrites!'

I stood in front of the Kop and flicked the Vs at the crowd. It wasn't premeditated but I knew that my actions would get me away from a club that I didn't want to be at.

I looked across and saw David Batty ready to enter the field with the No. 4 board being held aloft. Wilkinson, not surprisingly, was bringing me off. As I approached the dugout, he offered me a training top and ordered me to sit down. I told him to go and f*** himself and I ran straight down the tunnel to the dressing room. I knew my Leeds United career was over.

Wilkinson was furious. It was a serious breach of discipline and the die was cast. Aizlewood left for Bradford City during the summer.

Just as one midfielder came to the end of his time at Elland Road, another was on the launching pad for his own career.

Gary Speed had joined Leeds as a fourteen-year-old and had been working his way through the ranks. Wilkinson spotted something in him and gave him an early opportunity.

'I watched him play left-back in a youth game,' recalled the manager. 'After working with him in training a few times I was soon telling him he could play in a few other roles, most notably wide left and left midfield. I think by the end at Leeds, I'd played him in nine or ten outfield positions but, unlike some players, Gary never complained, never, ever showed any dissent. He just got on with things and, whatever job he was asked to do, invariably did it very well.'

Wilkinson blooded the nineteen-year-old against Oldham a few days after Aizlewood's show of temper. He was still raw but did enough to convince Wilkinson he could make it.

Things were starting to come together nicely for the manager. He knew that in Strachan he had the man to lead the team he would build and had come to a conclusion about where he needed to strengthen.

CHAPTER TWELVE

The Big Push

Just as a bright new future beckoned for Leeds United, the memory of each and every person connected with the club was dragged back to times gone by.

Less than a fortnight after the Whites signed off the 1988/89 season with a 3-3 draw at Shrewsbury, it was announced that former manager Don Revie had lost his battle against the incurable wasting illness that had crippled him.

Twelve months earlier, Elland Road had hosted a charity football match to raise money for research into motor neurone disease. It was Revie's final public appearance, sat for the most part in a wheelchair as all his old players gathered to pay their respects. Those who attended were shocked to witness the impact of the disease on Revie, now a shell of the man who had developed a team that was among the finest in Europe.

The poignant news of Revie's passing took everyone back to those glory days. Howard Wilkinson, for his part, was determined to bring back the success achieved under Revie's leadership. Away from the public gaze, he turned his attention to the next phase of the reconstruction of Leeds United.

Wilkinson's track record was enviable. His first full seasons in charge at both Notts County and Sheffield Wednesday brought promotion to the First Division. His promising first few months at Leeds gave every hint that he would complete the hat-trick in 1989/90.

The signings of Gordon Strachan and Chris Fairclough had shown the way – Wilkinson had no time for any slow burn rebuilding job and set his stall out for a no-holds-barred assault on the Second Division. He had been given a commitment by the directors that they would back his vision with cold, hard cash and now he took them at their word, splashing out big style.

Leeds spent £3.1 million on incoming transfers. Even the recovery of £1.7 million on those Wilkinson considered superfluous meant a net transfer deficit of £1.4 million, a massive show of faith by the board. It pushed the overdraft back up to £1 million and such a gamble demanded that Wilkinson delivered promotion.

In came John McClelland, John Hendrie, Mel Sterland, Chris O'Donnell, Mickey Thomas and Jim Beglin but the headlines were almost entirely devoted to the signing of Wimbledon hardman Vinnie Jones.

Jones was universally derided as a thug, a former hod carrier with little genuine talent. The £650,000 transfer was slated as folly, one which most predicted would blow up in Wilkinson's face.

Jones had a fearsome reputation, but there was method to Wilkinson's madness. He needed someone who could sort out the dressing room and Jones certainly did that.

Wilkinson: 'I made a lot of enquiries about Vinnie ... My feelings were that this was a bloke where there was more there than met the eye ... I'm not saying we didn't early doors have to just sort out a couple of things but after that there was no danger of him other than going out and playing and doing well and actually becoming a footballer that surprised a lot of people including many of his critics.'

Gordon Strachan was as apprehensive as anybody when Jones arrived. He and Wilkinson were scathing in their condemnation after Jones gave an Anderlecht player a bloody nose in a preseason friendly – the manager read the riot act and it had the necessary impact.

Strachan took a liking to Jones when he got beneath the thuggish front. The two men quickly became brothers in arms, both acutely conscious of the damaging split in the dressing room.

As Jones recalled, 'I discovered an element that was small-minded ... and anything but big-time. Quite a few new signings had been made including Gordon Strachan, Chris Fairclough, Mel Sterland and Mickey Thomas. Youngsters like David Batty, Gary Speed and Simon Grayson were on the brink of breaking into the side. But there were others like Ian Baird, Bobby Davison, Mark Aizlewood, John Sheridan and Brendon Ormsby who didn't seem sure about where they stood and they'd formed a bit of a clique. A big changeover in personnel was taking place and I had arrived in the middle of a situation where there were clearly two camps.'

Wilkinson made it clear that several players were persona non grata, telling them they should go find new clubs. Strachan went even further, confiding in Jones that 'it's a case of us against them'.

Jones: 'He gave me the kind of look I took to mean I should do something about it. I had become almost paranoid about eating my food, hearing them whispering and sniggering, and one day I'd had enough. I just leapt to my feet and confronted Davison.'

Davison was completely taken aback, pleading with Jones that 'You've got the wrong end of the stick.' Jones would have none of it, having sat through weeks of underlying tension and snide comments. The die was cast and he gave Davison a 'smack in the mouth' before turning on the others and snarling, 'This all stops, right here and now. If any of you want to say anything or do anything, here I am.'

Jones was bouncing, the adrenaline flowing, but feared that he might have gone too far. He feared the worst when he was summoned to Wilkinson's office but was in no mood to apologise, readying himself for a verbal set-to. He was caught completely off-guard by Wilkinson's calm response.

'You've disappointed me a bit, son. I've just been down to the players' lounge. Can't find one speck of blood in there.'

The intervention had been exactly what the manager had been hoping for when he signed Jones, a graphic demonstration of the need for togetherness, one which was unmistakable in its message.

Jones was a big personality, a genuine leader in the dressing room and another was the fast-raiding right-back Mel Sterland, whom Wilkinson had worked with at Sheffield Wednesday. Sterland, always referred to as 'Zico', was famous for his energetic attacking bursts and normally finished with an accurate cross or a blistering shot. His energy down the right earned him an England cap just before he left Wednesday for Rangers in Scotland in March. The move north of the border was a failure, thanks to a famous falling-out with manager Graeme Souness. He was with the Ibrox club for less than four months.

Sterland was delighted to be reunited with his old mentor and enjoyed a wonderful season with his perpetual blitzing of the right flank.

Before the season started, Aspin, Aizlewood, Rennie, Sheridan and Stiles had gone. There was disquiet at the departure of Sheridan, a massive favourite with the fans, but Wilkinson knew his mind and would not countenance any argument. Sheridan, with his lackadaisical approach to discipline and timekeeping, jarred badly with Wilkinson's template.

Physiotherapist Alan Sutton: 'The problem he had was Shez would never ever be a Howard Wilkinson kind of person. The day Howard Wilkinson walked in here on the Monday, Shez didn't even bother turning up for training ... He probably had a few over the weekend and Billy could handle that whereas Howard Wilkinson wasn't having that kind of culture.'

In contrast, Bobby Davison chose to stay and buckled down from the off. He profited in the early months of the season, his goals key. In his first nineteen appearances, he scored ten times. It was just as well with striking partner Ian Baird having a lean time in front of goal.

Jones was missing from the line-up for the opening day, away to Newcastle, with injury, but played in every game thereafter, an imposing presence alongside Strachan and David Batty in a midfield that dominated the division.

That first game at St James' Park saw Leeds suffer a chastening 5-2 defeat. Unsurprisingly, with five men given debuts, they were still getting to know each other, and it showed. It wasn't that they played poorly, in fact they bossed the first half, recovering from falling behind to an eighteenth-minute penalty to take a 2-1 lead, which they held at the interval.

Unfortunately, a succession of defensive errors saw United collapse in the second half with debutant Newcastle striker Micky Quinn enjoying a storming debut. Within two minutes of the resumption, he had equalised. He took his total haul on to four as United faltered – everything went for Quinn that day.

There was no panicking from Wilkinson, who kept any criticism behind closed doors. Forthright observations were spat out in the dressing room at the end but Wilkinson dismissed it publicly as teething difficulties. 'The second-half goals were a joke from our point of view,' he said. 'But the players know what I think and they think the same themselves. We defended very generously.'

Over the course of the next couple of games, Wilkinson sorted out his personnel.

Jim Beglin, who won the double with Liverpool in 1986, was still recovering from a preseason knee injury and clearly hadn't been ready at St James' Park. Wilkinson took him out of the firing line for the next game and then sent him out on loan to Plymouth for three months to recover his fitness. In the meantime, Mike Whitlow monopolised the left-back spot.

John McClelland also went by the wayside, replaced by the fit again Chris Fairclough, while Mickey Thomas quickly gave way to Vinnie Jones. The Welsh midfielder played in the first three games but was taken off in each one. He never appeared for United again and was gone to Stoke City before the end of the season.

Hendrie remained an automatic choice until he was stretchered off after a horrendous challenge by Swindon defender Jon Gittens in September. The two-footed lunge was barbaric, sending the Scot flying. He missed months of action, his place taken by midfielder Andy Williams.

Wilkinson's confidence was fully vindicated as his reshaped team went undefeated in the Second Division until mid-November, making themselves a fixture in the leading pack. Sheffield United, however, threatened to run away with the title, establishing a clear early lead at the top.

The resilience of Wilko's new Leeds was emphasised by victory at West Ham in early October. The two teams were a point apart in a tight promotion chase and the game became the obvious beacon for all the London press with the First Division programme postponed to give the England squad time to prepare for an important World Cup qualifier against Poland.

The hacks witnessed an iron-hard Leeds display in which they saw off the Hammers courtesy of a wonderful goal from Jones. Leeds' first win in the capital in four years saw them rise to third but the media painted it all as a throwback to the days of Dirty Leeds, much to Wilkinson's annoyance. He gave them short shrift, and when Leeds followed up by beating second-placed Sunderland, they were suddenly level on points with Sheffield United.

United remained rock solid within the automatic positions despite November defeats at Leicester and West Bromwich. A 3-0 success against Brighton on 16 December was their thirteenth victory in seventeen games – real promotion form. A two-goal victory at Middlesbrough a week earlier had taken them to the top of the table for the first time.

Keen on bolstering the promotion charge, Wilkinson dipped into the transfer market in January, paying out £400,000 for Nottingham Forest striker Lee Chapman, with whom he had worked for four years at Sheffield Wednesday.

Ian Baird, elected the club's player of the year only months earlier, took the signing as an indication that Wilkinson had no faith in him. The pair fell out badly and Baird demanded a transfer. He had been struggling for goals, but Wilkinson did all he could to keep him on board, even offering an improved contract. Baird, a cult favourite with the fans for his wholehearted displays, rejected the manager's pleas. He moved to Middlesbrough in a £500,000 deal after fifty-eight goals in 190 appearances over two separate spells at Elland Road. To compensate, Wilkinson brought in another Wednesday acquaintance, striker Imre Varadi.

Also on the way out was defender Noel Blake, sold to Stoke for a fee of £175,000. The deal included defender/midfielder Chris Kamara as a £150,000 makeweight after he chose Leeds in preference to Middlesbrough. Kamara provided cover for Sterland, who suffered a serious injury against Blackburn in January, and a still maturing David Batty when he suffered a late-season blip.

Chapman was an instant success – he scored on his debut as Leeds won 2-1 at Blackburn to increase their lead at the top to four points. It was their first win in six games and there were only two victories from the next seven fixtures as Leeds stuttered. Crucially, however, they retained a three-point lead at the top as Sheffield United suffered their own loss of form, compounded by a backlog of fixtures as they made their way into the sixth round of the FA Cup.

Chapman failed to score in a see-saw 4-3 defeat of Hull on 10 February, but Strachan and Hendrie each netted for a third successive game. Leeds were twice ahead, the second goal coming from a 30-yard dipping volley by Jones, only for Hull to equalise on both occasions. When the resilient Tigers snatched a 3-2 advantage with twelve minutes to go, shudders of anxiety filled Elland Road. Leeds struggled to impose their will on their relegation-threatened visitors until Strachan took hold of the game. He laid a third goal on a plate for Varadi and in stoppage time his chip over the advancing keeper found the top corner to settle the outcome.

Chapman's two goals earned a draw at Ipswich and he was on the scoresheet again in a 2-2 draw a week later, at home to West Brom in front of a 30,000 crowd.

Leeds' four-point lead was halved on 3 March as the Blades won 4-1 at Bradford City while Leeds lost at Watford and they were then held to a goalless draw by Port Vale. Sheffield United, with two games in hand, were doggedly hunting Leeds down. Momentum seemed to be with the South Yorkshire side.

Leeds' slump was ended when two further Chapman goals made the difference in a 4-2 victory at Oxford. Another brace from the striker gave Leeds a two-goal lead against West Ham. The advantage was halved by Trevor Morley but Strachan's fifteenth goal of the season made it 3-1. The Hammers scored again in the sixty-eighth minute but couldn't come again. Leeds held out for a 3-2 victory that maintained their four-point advantage over Sheffield United, who brushed aside sixth-placed Wolves 3-0.

Now Leeds went for it in earnest. A Sterland goal secured victory at Sunderland and then Jones and Chapman did the business at home to Portsmouth – the lead at the top was suddenly up to ten points, though the Blades retained two matches in hand. Over that same week, Sheffield had collapsed 5-0 at West Ham and then lost 2-1 at home to Barnsley. The fans were starting to celebrate with nine games left.

Suddenly, the tide changed. Just as Leeds seemed to be running away with the title, something got to them and the next four games yielded a mere two points. Now, the two Uniteds were tied on 75 points with five games remaining. With the two sides pitched against each other on Easter Monday, the Whites' nerves were jangling.

Elland Road housed the biggest crowd of the season outside the First Division – 32,727 – and there was a tense atmosphere as the game began, though Leeds quickly established their ascendancy. The Blades survived an almighty goalmouth scramble after goalkeeper Simon Tracey dropped the ball from a Jones cross and then Davison and Chapman each saw efforts desperately blocked. The pressure was soon to pay off.

Gary Speed, by now a fixture in the No. 11 shirt, sent Strachan clear, only for the Leeds skipper to be denied when Tracey dived at his feet. The ball squirted away to Kamara, whose low shot was blocked on the line by Paul Stancliffe. The rebound fell perfectly for Strachan, barely a yard out, to poke Leeds ahead.

Now, pre-match instructions from Howard Wilkinson began to take effect. He had singled out Tracey as a weak spot and instructed the players to pressurise him. 'I did it in a bid to affect the direction of his kicks because they were very important to Sheffield United,' Wilkinson explained. 'I told my strikers to make sure that if they stood up on Tracey to stand 4 yards off him so there could be no possibility of the referee deeming that they were deliberately trying to obstruct his kicks.'

One of the keeper's attempted clearances struck the back of Lee Chapman and went for a throw. Leeds regained possession and Speed made ground down the left before sending in a wonderful low cross. It flew past Tracey to be converted at the far post by a sliding Chapman for his eleventh goal for Leeds.

Eight minutes later, another Tracey error saw him kick the ball against Davison, whom he was then forced to bring down. Strachan duly rattled home the inevitable penalty.

The game was not yet done. Kamara came out of a challenge with the ball to free Speed at halfway. The winger raced in on goal, inspiring the iconic commentary, 'Go on Gary Speed, get one yourself, son.' As Stansfield closed on him, Speed fired left-footed into the bottom corner.

The crowd's celebration was ecstatic with the job almost done. With two automatic promotion places on offer and four games left, it appeared a foregone conclusion that Leeds (78 points) would be going up with either Sheffield United or Newcastle (both 75) condemned to the lottery of the play-offs. The widening of Leeds' goal difference advantage on Sheffield gave them an added boost.

But logic has rarely made much sense in the history of Leeds United and Wilkinson's men suddenly stumbled.

On 21 April, as Newcastle drew at Plymouth and Sheffield United beat Port Vale, Leeds slipped to a draw at Brighton, allowing the Blades to close to within a point.

Worse still, on 25 April, with Sheffield enjoying an evening off, Leeds contrived to lose 2-1 at home to twenty-first-placed Barnsley.

Everything seemed to be going to plan when Chris Fairclough, who had earlier received ten stitches in a head wound, threw himself at a Sterland cross to give Leeds the lead. Barnsley desperately needed points to avoid falling into the relegation zone and had little to lose. Manager Mel Machin shook things up, replacing both centre-backs – the impact was instant. The two subs, Brendan O'Connell and Owen Archdeacon, each scored in the space of eight second-half minutes to gift Barnsley an unexpected lead. The stadium was in despair at the startling change in fortunes.

Newcastle couldn't take full advantage, as they were held to a goalless draw at St James' Park by Swindon. Two points now covered the three sides, with Sheffield, a point behind Leeds, enjoying a game in hand.

32,597 crammed into Elland Road for the visit of Leicester City, anxiously waiting to see if Leeds could get back on track. Frayed nerves were eased early on by Sterland's blistering drive for 1-0 and the goal still separated the sides at the interval. In the second half, however, United's ragged nerves got the better of them as Leicester carved out several chances before Gary McAllister equalised with a spectacular effort. Minutes later, McAllister went close again with another fierce 30-yard strike parried away by Mervyn Day. With both Sheffield United and Newcastle winning, things looked bleak.

Cue Gordon Strachan and a momentous goal. There were six minutes remaining when Sterland's long throw sparked panic in the Leicester box. McAllister prodded the ball out of the immediate danger zone but Speed chested the ball into Strachan's path. In a moment that was to assume legendary proportions, the United captain fired home left-footed to send the crowd into epic scenes, one part relief to three parts triumph.

'Did you ever see a better goal? And did you ever see one better timed?' Commentator John Helm's words became folklore as Strachan seized victory.

With Newcastle being held at home by West Ham, Strachan's goal could have clinched promotion but the Geordies bagged a late winner to take the promotion race to the final day. Sheffield United hammered Bournemouth 4-2 to maintain their own push but missed their chance to go clear at the top three days later when they finished goalless at Blackburn. Now, they and Leeds were locked together on 82 points.

As the season came to a shuddering conclusion on 5 May, the big three could all win the title, although Newcastle, two points in arrears, were outsiders.

All three sides were away, Leeds on the south coast at Bournemouth, Newcastle facing a North East derby at Middlesbrough and Sheffield United travelling to Leicester. Added spice was brought to matters with Middlesbrough (47 points) and Bournemouth (48) locked in a struggle to avoid being the third side to accompany long-gone Bradford City and Stoke into the Third Division. With Leicester having nothing to play for, the Blades had a slim psychological advantage but their goal difference was inferior by nine to Leeds and eleven to Newcastle.

On the hottest May day since records began, the only first-half goals came at Leicester, where the home side took an early lead. The 10,000 travelling Blades fans were shell-shocked, though it would still take a Newcastle victory to deny them. They were soon in seventh heaven when Paul Wood nipped in at the far post to equalise.

The spur of a goal had Sheffield on top form and Brian Deane bundled home from close range after Ian Bryson and Tony Agana saw shots blocked on the line.

Agana and Wilf Rostron made it 4-1 only for Leicester to pull one back before the interval. If the scores remained as they were, the Blades would go up as champions.

Down at Dean Court, Leeds were having the better of a nervy, edgy contest but news of Sheffield's lead rattled them. Anxiety gave way to ecstasy as the game moved into the second half. Chris Kamara whipped over a delicious cross from the right that screamed, 'Head me in.' Lee Chapman's eyes lit up and he duly obliged, powering a trademark header past Bournemouth keeper Gerry Peyton. The United contingent in the crowd went mental, baying their glee. It was as if eight years of depression and decline were obliterated with that one instinctive move.

Bournemouth were on the ropes as they slipped into the relegation zone. They simply had no way back against a side that swelled with passion and pride. One sensed that no team could have denied Leeds that day. What Bournemouth spirit remained vanished as the news came through that Middlesbrough were running riot against Newcastle. Ian Baird was doing his former employers a big favour as Boro rubbed in their superiority.

Almost as soon as Chapman scored, Boro did the same, main man Bernie Slaven stabbing home from a Paul Kerr cross. Six minutes later it was two as Slaven squared for Baird to prod into the open goal.

Newcastle pulled one back after seventy minutes but Baird was on hand to restore the two-goal cushion. They finished it off with a fourth in injury-time, but by then Leeds were out of sight at the top, taking the championship on goal difference as the travelling fans poured onto the pitch to celebrate a famous victory.

The Leeds players came out to acknowledge the supporters before a riotous champagne celebration in the dressing room. While the party continued all the way back to Yorkshire, thousands headed for the beach to toast the win – after eight tortuous, depressing, turgid years, Leeds were back in the big time and didn't everybody know it.

CHAPTER THIRTEEN

In the Limelight and Loving It

There were questions in the House in the days following Leeds United's title-winning victory on the south coast. The damage wreaked by ill-behaved supporters in Bournemouth that bank holiday weekend shocked everybody and there had to be a reckoning.

Trouble at United games had diminished significantly since Howard Wilkinson took the managerial reins and events over the weekend were as unexpected as they were shocking, though there were plenty of 'told you so's spouted in the days following the trouble.

Thousands upon thousands of Leeds fans headed to Dorset for the weekend, many without tickets. Ahead of the game, an estimated 5,500 Whites followers basked in sweltering temperatures in their T-shirts and shorts, with thousands more watching the action back in West Yorkshire on a TV beam-back.

The night before the game there had been serious trouble with the police and Bournemouth was seething with tension, pre-match clashes stoking up the temperature. That was as nothing next to the post-match devastation inflicted on the sleepy seaside resort.

'We, the players, want to make one thing clear,' said Gordon Strachan. 'The lads at Elland Road have won this championship not for the troublemakers but for the genuine, well-behaved supporters who have backed us in the right manner. Unfortunately, there are a few hundred morons – and that is what they are, morons – who tarnish the name of the club with their actions. If those people think the championship is theirs, then they should think again. And they can call me what they like for that.'

'I'm not sure who scheduled the fixtures,' said teammate John Hendrie, 'but Bournemouth away for Leeds United on the last day of the season on a Bank Holiday weekend wasn't very smart. Bournemouth is like an old folks' paradise and Dean Court was a tiny ground.'

Home Secretary David Waddington spoke three days later in the House of Commons:

> There was serious disorder in the town over the entire weekend, mainly involving Leeds supporters. To date, 104 arrests have been made and criminal damage totalling around £40,000 has been reported. Many police officers were hurt, and twelve received serious injuries.
>
> The scenes of violent disorder witnessed in Bournemouth were absolutely disgraceful ... Serious disorder was anticipated by the police at Bournemouth and repeated requests were made to the football authorities to reschedule the fixture, the first such request being made as long ago as last June. It is for the football authorities to explain why they did not respond positively to those requests. I have called in both the Football League and the Football Association to discuss the matter, and I will be seeing the League later today, and possibly a representative of the Football Association. It is high time that the football authorities heeded rather than ignored sensible advice.

Seeking to deflect the attention away from their poor judgement in scheduling the match, the football authorities declared themselves so disturbed by the trouble that they might render United's promotion null and void. Leslie Silver and the Leeds board feared the worst; in the end, the FA relented, but warned the club that any further problems would result in four games having to be played behind closed doors and any further repetition would lead to expulsion from the FA, with all that implied.

Given the all-clear, Howard Wilkinson began his preparations for the First Division with some judicious strengthening. Much of his attention over the previous eighteen months had been on bolstering the spine of the side – in addition to bringing in Strachan as leader, he had recruited steel down the middle with Chris Fairclough, Vinnie Jones and Lee Chapman. Appreciating that it would need more than steel to cope with the top flight, he spent big in the summer to bring in John Lukic, Chris Whyte and Gary McAllister.

Goalkeeper Lukic broke through as a teenager at Leeds in the late 1970s before moving to Arsenal in a £125,000 deal in 1983. His value had risen to £1 million by the time he left Highbury for a sentimental return to Elland Road.

Gangling centre-back Whyte had begun his career at Arsenal and spent a couple of years in the United States before returning to England with a move to West Bromwich Albion in 1988. Wilkinson saw him as the perfect partner for Fairclough and met Albion's asking price of £450,000.

But the big signing was Leicester and Scotland midfielder McAllister, who had come so close to destroying his new team's promotion chances when he equalised at Elland Road in April. The Scot was a rare talent, catching the eye of many for the range of his passing, and it was a feather in the cap of Bill Fotherby that McAllister agreed to throw in his lot with Leeds.

To seal the million-pound deal, Fotherby was forced to throw in the Mercedes that he was driving at the time – it wasn't actually his to give, but that was mere detail for Fotherby.

Wilkinson had pointed Fotherby in McAllister's direction but knew that it was a long shot, that others would be courting the elegant schemer. He couldn't believe his luck when Fotherby rang up at midnight to break the good news. Merry with wine, all Wilkinson could utter when he heard was a sceptical 'F*** off'.

The signings of Lukic, Whyte and McAllister were bad news for Mervyn Day, Peter Haddock and Vinnie Jones, the obvious contenders to make way for the new men – Haddock continued to figure in various positions until his career was ended by injury a few months later and Day hung around for another three years as a dutiful reserve. It was a different story with Jones, who was quickly off, making just one further appearance before quitting for a reunion with former Wimbledon manager Dave Bassett at Sheffield United.

Jones was heartbroken by the course of events – he had become a cult favourite with the Elland Road fans and always regretted not having a lengthier stay at the club. His desire to retain the No. 4 shirt saw him light-heartedly pointing a 12-bore shotgun in Wilkinson's general direction. 'Are you sure, boss?'

Despite the strengthening, there was apprehension amongst fans about how Leeds would cope with the challenge of top-flight football, with most hoping merely that they could stay up. They need not have worried – Wilkinson had steered both Notts County and Sheffield Wednesday safely through the choppy waters of the First Division and knew what was required. He had Leeds up and running from day one.

United's return to the First Division brought a baptism of fire – away to Everton.

The Toffees were no longer the outstanding side led to prominence by Howard Kendall in the mid-1980s, but they still represented a major challenge for a promoted side.

Kendall had inspired a golden age for the Goodison club with two league titles and success in both FA Cup and Cup Winners' Cup. In the aftermath of the ban on English clubs competing in Europe, Kendall quit for Athletic Bilbao. Assistant manager Colin Harvey replaced him but couldn't match Kendall's achievements. Nevertheless, he led Everton to three solid top-eight finishes and they were hotly backed to beat Leeds, whom many critics suggested would face a relegation struggle.

In the event, Leeds surprised many with the quality of their football and took an early lead. There were eight minutes on the clock when Everton failed to clear their lines following a long throw by David Batty into their area. As the ball bounced into the 6-yard area, Fairclough took advantage to nod home unchallenged.

Everton had their moments in the first half and were awarded a penalty when Fairclough was adjudged to have handled as he challenged Graeme Sharp for a high ball. Neil McDonald blasted his spot kick wide in front of the massed ranks of away fans and Leeds breathed a heavy sigh of relief.

The Whites enjoyed a decent amount of possession and eagerly snapped into tackles, bullying Everton in midfield. They enjoyed further reward four minutes before the break after Everton were undone by a massive kick downfield from Lukic. Goalkeeper Neville Southall and Martin Keown crashed into each other as they struggled to beat Imre Varadi to the ball and Speed calmly swept home the loose ball.

Partly in frustration at Everton's lacklustre first-half display, Southall launched a high-profile one-man protest. The big Welshman had been a mainstay of the 1980s glory and he was so disillusioned by Everton's downwards trajectory that he had demanded a transfer in the summer. His request had been rejected and a poor first half had been the straw that broke the camel's back – his frustration boiled over and prompted a very visible display of his disaffection. He came out long before his teammates at the start of the second half, sitting angrily against the foot of his post.

Everton pushed strongly at the start of the half but on the hour Leeds opened a three-goal lead when Varadi lashed home from 3 yards when Everton could not handle Speed's shot.

Everton staged a late fightback with goals from Pat Nevin and John Ebbrell but United hung on for a victory that caught the media by surprise.

Three days later, Leeds were on top note again with a goalless draw at home to a strong Manchester United side. A 3-0 hammering of Norwich the following weekend saw them up to second behind Liverpool as the country held its breath at the way they dealt with some of the best clubs in the land.

Their opening burst was ended by defeats against Luton and Spurs. The Whites bounced back with a victory at Sheffield United but then failed to win again in the league until 3 November when goals from Chapman, Strachan and McAllister saw off Nottingham Forest at Elland Road. The goal was Chapman's fifth in the league as he proved himself as adept in the top flight as he had been in the Second Division. He scored in each of the next four games as Leeds began to find their feet properly, a flurry of victories taking them fifth.

Leeds saw out 1990 with a draw at Old Trafford followed by five straight victories as an unbeaten run stretched to fourteen. Including cup competitions, Chapman's goal haul now stood at thirteen, already the highest by a Leeds player in the First Division since John Hawley's sixteen in

1978/79. The quality of McAllister's contribution to United's midfield, now talked up as the country's best, was a decisive factor in their climb.

The New Year began poorly, with Leeds defeated 3-0 at Liverpool and then 2-0 at Norwich. Wilkinson and Co. reacted with equanimity, clicking back into the sort of form that embedded them as fixtures in the top four. They also proved durable opponents in the cup competitions: Arsenal needed four attempts to put them out in the FA Cup at the fourth-round stage, while they worked their way through to the semi-finals of the Rumbelows Cup where they met Manchester United.

The week before the first leg at Old Trafford, Lee Chapman suffered an excruciating injury in a goalless draw at Tottenham. Chapman was caught in the face by the boot of Steve Sedgley and went tumbling face first into the cinder track around the pitch. He was spark out and physio Alan Sutton was clearly concerned as he frantically tended to his injuries. His face had been ripped apart, his nose broken in two places, and it required 100 stitches, plastic surgery and super glue to repair the damage. Amazingly, Chapman lined up against the Red Devils a few days later, bruised and battered but determined to play.

Manchester won the game 2-1 and finished the job with a single-goal victory at Elland Road.

Leeds had also made it through to the two-legged Northern Area Final of the Full Members Cup against Everton, but they missed out on a Wembley final despite two goals from Chapman in the first leg. He managed two more in a 5-0 victory against Sunderland that sustained their push in the league and went even further in a top-four battle with second-placed Liverpool at Elland Road on 13 April.

Howard Wilkinson was hoping for a win to reduce the nine-point gap between the two sides but got his tactical calls all wrong. He hoped to exploit a lack of a defensive midfielder in the Liverpool line-up, ordering his defence to play a high back line and crowd the Reds' midfield. Leeds started quickly and had some early success but the tide quickly began to turn. The Whites lost their rhythm as they began to surrender possession through inaccurate passing. Liverpool found the acres of space behind the Leeds back four much to their liking and used the through ball to perfection.

Ian Rush and John Barnes had outstanding games, carving Leeds open with intelligent football that made the Leeds defence look ponderous.

Liverpool simply tore Leeds apart in the first thirty minutes, netting four times without reply. According to United writer Jon Howe, 'On 28 minutes Barnes played a one-two on the halfway line with Rush and then, showing pace I didn't know he possessed, left Whyte and Fairclough in his wake as he bore down on Lukic and nonchalantly drilled the ball passed him [for Liverpool's fourth]. At this point pockets of Leeds fans around the ground burst into spontaneous applause, it was pointless denying it, this was football of a class we hadn't seen for many years. We were on the ropes and ripe for a severe beating.'

It was a different story after the break, with Liverpool settling for what they had and Barnes badly feeling the pace of the first period. Leeds' full-backs came strongly into the game, providing the ammunition for Chapman to find his aerial game.

The tide had turned but it took a while for Leeds to make their new momentum count. Midway through the half, Chapman fired home after a McAllister shot was blocked. Then the big striker powered home a header from a steepling ball into the area, but the referee chalked the effort off for a foul on goalkeeper Mike Hooper.

A minute later, Shutt turned nicely to fire home United's second after a throw by Speed. Liverpool responded instantly, Barnes taking a back heel from Rush before outpacing the Leeds defence to make it 5-2.

Any normal side would have called it a day and limited their ambition to avoiding further humiliation. But a never-say-die United were not done and continued to pour forward – within two minutes Chapman had nodded their third from a cross by Batty.

Leeds surged forward in pursuit of the unlikeliest of draws. Strachan wriggled his way through the Liverpool box before chipping to the far post. There was Chapman again, leaping to nod home for his hat-trick.

Still the Whites came on, but a fifth goal was beyond them.

The 5-4 defeat was a moral victory after such a devastating first half and the fans trooped away into the night after one of the most incredible matches ever staged at the stadium. Chapman's goal haul took him onto seventeen in the league and twenty-seven in all competitions. He notched another four in the remaining five games. Leeds lost twice but three victories secured a fourth-place finish, their highest since 1974. Chapman missed out by one goal to Alan Smith of champions Arsenal in the race to be top scorer in the First Division. Smith's hat-trick in the penultimate game, a 3-1 defeat of Manchester United, saw him seal the deal.

Chapman was one of five United players who started all thirty-eight First Division games, Lukic, Sterland, Whyte and McAllister matching him. As good a season as it was for the towering striker, his captain, Gordon Strachan, impressed even more, being elected Footballer of the Year. His consistency and inspirational leadership was key in helping Leeds find their feet at the top level.

Howard Wilkinson's face barely changed from week to week but inside he was well-satisfied with the progress made. His ten-year plan remained on track.

CHAPTER FOURTEEN

Rosettes and Roast Lamb

The ease with which Leeds United got to grips with the First Division astonished many. Certainly, it convinced Leslie Silver, Bill Fotherby and Howard Wilkinson that the sky was the limit. Wilkinson's initial conviction that Leeds could win the championship 'within five or six years' now seemed a realistic aim rather than overblown ambition. The speed of their ascent surprised even their most ardent admirers.

Eager to strike while the iron was hot, a delighted board backed Wilkinson to the hilt. There were some big names coming in (Steve Hodge, Rod Wallace and Tony Dorigo) and some not so big names (Rod's brother Ray and young Sheffield Wednesday defenders David Wetherall and Jon Newsome). There were few departures and undoubtedly the squad was stronger for Wilkinson's tweaking.

Steve Hodge was the biggest name; the former England midfielder had been in the side that lost to Argentina in the 1986 World Cup – Diego Maradona, the Hand of God and all that – and had enjoyed an illustrious club career with Aston Villa, Spurs and Forest. Even at £900,000, he looked a good buy, though it was difficult to see how Wilkinson would shoehorn him into the side other than as cover for an ageing Strachan.

The biggest fee was the £1.6 million demanded by Southampton for striker Rod Wallace, who was accompanied by twin brother Ray as a £100,000 add-in. The pair's other brother, Danny, quit Southampton in September 1989 for an inconsequential spell at Manchester United.

The biggest value came with the £1.3 million paid to Chelsea for Australian left-back Tony Dorigo, a member of England's 1990 World Cup squad as reserve to Stuart Pearce. Dorigo's attacking flair would become a feature of United's play over the years to come. At a stroke, Wilkinson had solved his left-back problem. Over his three years at the helm, he had tried various players in the position, but none had fully met his exacting standards.

With the sale of 20,000 season tickets generating £3.5 million up front and the prospect of high television and broadcasting income to come, the board considered the £4.2 million spent on transfers as a sound investment. There was a hint, though, of a gambler's punt about Wilkinson's moves, betraying his maxim that only one out of every three transfers ever paid off.

England manager Graham Taylor, Wilkinson's close friend, was in the Elland Road crowd when United kicked off their campaign against Nottingham Forest. Their opening day fixture against Crystal Palace had been delayed by building work at Selhurst Park, required to comply with FA regulations.

Wilkinson gave debuts to Dorigo and Rod Wallace but left Hodge and Mel Sterland on the bench.

Forest performed well and were somewhat lucky not to win with John Lukic forced into a fine display. It was Leeds who took the points, though, thanks to a thirteenth-minute goal from Gary McAllister, fired home from the edge of the area.

Hodge got his chance in the next game, as substitute for Gary Speed, and scored United's goal in a 1-1 draw with Sheffield Wednesday.

The season really took off with the following fixture, away to Southampton. The 4-0 victory was United's best ever at The Dell and showcased the quality of Speed, who contributed two classic goals, including the opener. Saints defender Neil Ruddock was sent off after fifty-six minutes for a foul on former teammate Wallace as he made for goal. Strachan converted the resultant penalty and he repeated his spot kick feat fourteen minutes later after a foul on Lee Chapman. Speed rounded off the rout with a 30-yard thunderbolt a minute from time.

This was Wilkinson's Leeds at full throttle: strong and unyielding at the back with Chris Whyte and Chris Fairclough smothering the threat of Alan Shearer and Matt Le Tissier; Sterland and Dorigo willing and adept raiders down the flanks, the former a rampaging force of nature, the other cultured and elegant with a fine touch and gorgeous left foot; Chapman a focal point up front, never giving the Saints rearguard a moment's peace, while Wallace buzzed around like an annoying wasp. The real difference between the sides, though, lay in midfield where Strachan, Batty, McAllister and Speed continued to push their claims of being the outstanding combination in the top flight.

Wilkinson was happy to pronounce it as a job well done as Leeds climbed to third, despite having played only three games to everybody else's four.

Now came the big test, against Alex Ferguson and his table-topping Manchester United side at a sun-soaked Old Trafford.

Everyone forecast a home win, but Leeds outdid themselves, quickly getting on the front foot. After seven minutes Strachan, McAllister and

Speed brought the ball out of defence to set up Chapman to power home a header at the back post after goalkeeper Peter Schmeichel misjudged Speed's cross. It was a typical Leeds move, clearing their lines and accurately finding their men with long passes. Some derided Wilko and his team as long-ball merchants but it was simply direct and economic football, perfect counter-attacking play.

Fergie's men had plenty of the ball, but Leeds looked capable of frustrating them until Bryan Robson managed to find a scrappy equaliser with five minutes left.

Wilkinson was disappointed not to take all three points, but Leeds moved on with a home draw against champions Arsenal and then a 3-0 blitzing of a high-flying Manchester City side. The crowd went wild as Batty scored the second, a goal rarer than hen's teeth.

Carl Shutt's strike was enough to see off Chelsea at Stamford Bridge as Leeds moved up to second, evidencing that they were serious title contenders. No one had expected this, but Leeds' play was effervescent and exciting, energetic and effective. Even a goalless draw at Coventry could not dislodge them from second as they prepared for a major challenge against a strong Liverpool side.

United gave another high-octane display to beat the Merseysiders for the first time since 1973. The only goal of the game came courtesy of Hodge, a surprise starter in midfield in place of Wallace. He hooked home after Bruce Grobbelaar failed to clear a Strachan corner and Dorigo fired the ball back in. It was probably the high point of Hodge's time at Leeds – he and Wilkinson fell out. The manager bemoaned Hodge's propensity for injury, while Hodge was unconvinced by Wilkinson's approach.

'In midfield we usually spent large parts of the game watching the ball sail over our heads,' Hodge wrote in his autobiography. 'From my earliest days at Forest, I'd always been taught that the game should be played on the ground. Crisp passing and quick movement. Play the game as it was meant to be played.' 'Isn't it terrible when you beat these passing teams?' crowed Wilkinson after a 1-0 win at West Ham.

Leeds secured the Liverpool victory with their sixth clean sheet in nine matches. After ten games, only they and Manchester United remained unbeaten. Leeds' record was spoiled on 1 October as they lost at Crystal Palace, but they snapped back with four-goal victories against Sheffield United and Notts County.

Every time a point was dropped, cynical media men would predict the bubble had burst but Wilkinson and Co. were simply not having it. The manager's practice was to set out the points he expected to get from blocks of games, the very antithesis of the hackneyed 'taking every game as it comes' maxim. The story was kept secret from the public and the media but the players were fully aware of it and suffered no ill effects as Leeds closely tracked the trajectory forecast by Wilkinson.

On 26 October, a single-goal defeat of Oldham took Leeds top for the first time since the days of Don Revie. They had played a game more than Manchester United but that was a mere technicality for their supporters, who crowed at their advantage over the despised Old Trafford side.

A month later came a crucial afternoon. A televised Sunday afternoon fixture at Villa Park gave the entire nation the chance to see exactly how good Leeds were and they delivered a tour de force performance.

It was not just the goals in the 4-1 victory, but the breathtaking nature of United's play that captivated the attention against an Aston Villa side that had won five games on the bounce.

With Gary Speed missing through injury, Wilkinson detailed Chris Fairclough to shadow Villa winger Tony Daley and snuff out his threat. John McClelland partnered Whyte in the centre of defence and Leeds adapted superbly with Strachan, McAllister and Batty dominating midfield.

There was only one goal in the first half, Wallace touching home after forty minutes when Chapman's header was saved.

Leeds ran riot after the break, the action starting a minute in when Sterland headed home at close range from a corner. Another corner ten minutes later took a different route but was just as effective with Strachan laying on an opening for Chapman in the 6-yard area.

Villa pulled one back when Yorke tapped home halfway through the half, but as the seconds ticked down Chapman threw himself full-length to power home Sterland's telling cross.

Wilkinson glowed with pride at the end, describing the game as one of the best performances of his managerial career. Most of the country had to agree, although Manchester United were still widely regarded as favourites for the title.

Wilkinson coolly disregarded the headlines, refusing to allow anyone at Elland Road to get carried away, but he knew that Leeds had it in them to go all the way. The team spirit and never-say-die attitude that he had engendered and Strachan had nurtured gave the players a deep and unquenchable confidence that they could overcome all the odds.

They required all their resilience as 1991 turned into 1992 with three games against Manchester United in the space of eighteen days — the two sides were pitched against each other in the fifth round of the Rumbelows Cup and the third round of the FA Cup following a league encounter at Elland Road on 29 December. Leeds went into the latter game in decent form, undefeated in the eleven First Division games since the beginning of October.

Neil Webb fired the Red Devils into the lead at the start of the second half with a half-volley from 25 yards following a corner. Manchester looked good for victory but with ten minutes remaining, Gary Pallister sent Gary McAllister flying in the area and the referee had no hesitation in awarding Leeds a penalty. Mel Sterland calmly sent Peter Schmeichel the wrong way from the spot as he stroked the ball into the other corner.

Leeds spent the rest of the game camped deep in the Manchester half but were unable to fashion a decent chance. They had to be satisfied with the point that kept them within two of the visitors, who had two games in hand. Leeds' lead on third-placed Sheffield Wednesday was seven.

It was a different story in the two cup encounters. Gary Speed gave Leeds the lead in the Rumbelows but Fergie's men responded comprehensively with goals from Clayton Blackmore, Andrei Kanchelskis and Ryan Giggs; in the FA Cup, a Mark Hughes goal a minute before the break was enough to settle the tie.

Mixed in with that spell there were some positive moments for Leeds. On New Year's Day, QPR unexpectedly won 4-1 at Old Trafford and when Leeds won 3-1 at West Ham that afternoon they went a point clear.

There was also another extraordinary performance for the television cameras when Wilkinson took his men to Sheffield Wednesday to meet his former club on 12 January. A Lee Chapman hat-trick was the highlight of a red-letter display that yielded a 6-1 victory. The rout began within nine minutes when Chapman swept home from close in after Fairclough nodded down a McAllister corner. Dorigo increased the lead, the Aussie's goal cracked home from 30 yards after Leeds were awarded a free kick.

Then came a truly bizarre episode deep inside the Leeds area. Chris Whyte tried to let Roland Nilsson's daisy-cutter run to Lukic, but Wednesday striker Gordon Watson intervened. He flicked the ball away and as it ran wide chose to take the most flamboyant of dives. He had taken a couple of paces away from Whyte before deciding to hurl himself skyward and then rolling theatrically for yards. For some reason known only to himself, the referee bought it and awarded a penalty. Leeds' players were astonished and Wilkinson exasperated at the most disgraceful and blatant of dives – Watson would always be pilloried for his cheating that day.

Former Leeds midfielder John Sheridan seemed to agree with his former teammates, his spot kick close enough for Lukic to turn it onto a post before he almost apologetically netted the rebound.

Their disgust seemed only to drive Leeds on and they blew Wilkinson's former team apart with four more spectacular goals.

The victory sent United twelve points clear of Wednesday and eleven above Liverpool, newly established as the third-placed side.

Leeds' smooth progress and Chapman's extraordinary productivity in front of goal were both undermined by an incident in the closing seconds of the final game of the triple header against Manchester United.

Leeds had been pressing hard for an equaliser and a peach of a cross came in from Mel Sterland. Chapman's eyes lit up and he moved in on a golden opportunity, but he was knocked off balance by a challenge from Gary Pallister and fell badly, his left harm under him and his wrist badly broken. He was taken to Leeds General Infirmary for an operation. It was feared he would be out for months and with him would go Leeds' chances of the title.

Wilkinson's initial solutions were less than transformative. First, he asked Gary Speed to fill in temporarily and then he brought in Notts County striker Tony Agana on a short-term loan that offered little. His more permanent solution was to have a seismic impact, not just for Leeds, but for English football as a whole.

Sheffield Wednesday, now managed by Trevor Francis, had offered a trial to a French international striker, Eric Cantona, but were umming and aahing about a deal. Cantona's career in France had been controversial and stormy and he had sought a new start in England after falling foul of French officialdom.

Francis was prepared to offer a permanent contract, but Wednesday quailed at the £1 million fee. They opted instead to try and agree a loan deal after a one-week trial, but Cantona refused to countenance the idea and it seemed that his opportunity of a comeback to top-flight football was gone.

Suddenly, Wilkinson came onto the scene to persuade Cantona to throw his lot in with Leeds. In a matter of days a deal was done and the Frenchman was on his way to West Yorkshire. Cantona signed at the beginning of February and sat alongside Wilkinson to watch the match against Notts County.

'Howard Wilkinson had been very clear with me from the first training sessions,' recalled Cantona. 'He was convinced that I could rapidly impose myself on Leeds United, but he also let me understand that he didn't want to push me too quickly. English clubs, it is true, display a certain distrust of foreign players. Their football is made out of aerial duels, of hard running and of tackles which cannot be endured unless a player's physical condition is almost perfect.'

The match against Notts ended in a 3-0 victory, which kept Leeds at the top of the league, but they dropped to second the following week when Cantona made his debut for Leeds in a 2-0 defeat at Oldham. He came on as a second-half substitute for Hodge but pulled up few trees.

Manchester United had not won a league title since 1967 but were looking more and more likely to end that run. They were getting the upper hand.

Cantona made his first start a couple of weeks later in a 1-1 draw at Everton and it was shortly afterwards that his stay at Leeds really took off, on 29 February, at home to Luton.

Cantona scored and Leeds won 2-1 to get back on track, but their form was very up and down. This was despite the return of Chapman, who had declared himself fit and ready to play with a plastic case on his damaged wrist. The Whites crashed 4-1 at QPR, then a goal from Cantona sparked off a 5-1 thrashing of Wimbledon, which featured a rip-roaring hat-trick from Chapman. But Leeds suddenly stuttered – there were a couple of draws and they were humbled by four goals at Manchester City. Many Leeds supporters gave up hope after that debacle on 4 April. It left Manchester United on top with three games in hand and odds-on favourites with the bookmakers.

But City were to have a further hand in matters. They flung Leeds an unexpected lifeline when they secured a 1-1 draw at Old Trafford the following Wednesday, coming from behind with a man short.

The Red Devils' continued progress in the Rumbelows Cup had created fixture congestion – they won the trophy the following week by beating Nottingham Forest at Wembley, but that was another game they still had to play, while Leeds were starting to run into form.

The previous day Leeds had won a momentous game against Chelsea as Cantona, on as a sub for Wallace, took centre stage.

Leeds dominated the game, but only had a goal at the start of the second half to show for their dominance. Desperate to get the second goal that would kill the game off, Wilkinson summoned Cantona from the bench with twenty minutes left to play. Almost immediately he set Chapman up to make it 2-0, and then came the coup de grace as Cantona gave the clearest evidence possible of what he could bring to the party.

'It is difficult to describe the out-of-the-ordinary goal that I scored on that day,' recalled the Frenchman. 'In three touches I deceived the defenders who were coming to tackle me, without the ball touching the ground and then finally placed the ball in the far corner of the net. About ten minutes remained and throughout the whole of that time the fans stood up in the stands, singing and chanting. It was a very moving and extraordinary experience.'

The moment would last as a memory at Elland Road for years, though in truth Cantona's was only a cameo contribution to Leeds' title drive. Wilkinson remained implacably unconvinced of his ability to improve the team's overall performance.

The Elland Road faithful, however, had no doubts. They had found a new folk hero and the chant of 'Ooh, aah, Cantona,' soon became a rallying cry as they gathered their forces for a final push. Cantona brought a flair that had been missing, an unmistakable *je ne sais quoi*.

As Leeds' star rose, a strange case of nerves settled on Old Trafford. The closeness of the title seemed to strike terror into their hearts and they entered a period of disastrous form. The home draw with City was followed by another, against relegation-threatened Luton.

The pressure seemed to wear more on the Manchester men than Leeds and Wilkinson was playing the game perfectly, on and off the pitch.

Alex Ferguson became legendary for his mind games over the next two decades, but they didn't work in 1992 as Wilkinson blanked both him and the media.

Ferguson insisted that the pressure was on Leeds because they'd not won anything. But the more vocal the Manchester United boss became, the less Wilkinson said. There was a feeling of serenity around Elland Road as their opponents imploded.

Nerves consumed Fergie's men when they lost 2-1 at home to Nottingham Forest on Easter Monday with young Irish midfielder Roy Keane bossing the game. Leeds, facing Coventry at Elland Road two hours later, took advantage with a 2-0 victory.

Manchester still had a game in hand against relegation-threatened West Ham at Upton Park. The Hammers hadn't registered a goal in their three defeats that preceded the game and it appeared to be a 'gimme'. However, it was the Red Devils' fourth game in seven days, as Ferguson would later complain to anyone that would listen. He also had to cope with a growing injury list and West Ham took advantage. Billy Bonds' men rose to the occasion, giving their supporters a rare good day at the office.

Midway through the second half, defender Kenny Brown smacked home a volley to give the Hammers a lead that Manchester could never wipe out and suddenly Leeds had their destiny in their own hands. Victories in their last two games would guarantee them the title. The only response from Old Trafford was a bizarre comment from Ferguson that the Hammers' performance was 'obscene' when set against their customary meek displays.

On Sunday 26 April, the television cameras captured the drama as Leeds took to the field early for an extraordinary Yorkshire derby, away to Sheffield United.

Alan Cork gave the Blades the lead, but fortune shone on Leeds. They snatched a fluky equaliser on the stroke of half-time, a Sheffield clearance cannoning first off Gary Speed and then against Rod Wallace's knee before finding the net.

Blades keeper Mel Rees was injured in the incident and his movement was hampered thereafter. He was unable to offer much resistance when a McAllister free kick was met at the far post by a headlong dive from Jon Newsome and Leeds were ahead.

The bizarre happenings continued as the Blades equalised courtesy of Lee Chapman's own goal when he could not get out of the way of John Pemberton's sharp cut back.

The author, sporting United's 1995 away shirt, enjoys a pre-game pint at Elland Road.

Allan Clarke following his appointment as Leeds manager, 18 September 1980.

Allan Clarke shows the strain in the Elland Road dugout during a victory against Crystal Palace, 25 October 1980.

Howard Wilkinson and Bill Fotherby in October 1988 as the new manager is revealed to the world.

Burley Banksy's street art tribute to Gary Speed and a famous quote from 1990.

Howard Wilkinson anxiously watches the crucial game at Bournemouth on 5 May 1992. Leslie Silver is to Wilkinson's right.

Vinnie Jones street art, painted by Tom Crowe of the Northern Mural Company, at Whingate Junction in Armley.

The Leeds United squad enjoying themselves preseason 1991/92 outside the Hard Rock Café in Tokyo. Back: Lee Chapman, John Lukic, Imre Varadi, Rod Wallace, Ray Wallace, David Wetherall, David Batty, Chris Whyte, John McClelland, Chris Fairclough, Bobby Davison. Front: Dylan Kerr, Tony Dorigo, Gary Speed. (© Gary Edwards)

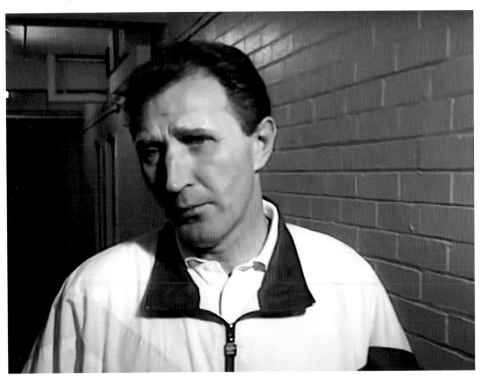

Howard Wilkinson in conversation with the press, 1992.

Howard Wilkinson a few days before Leeds' vital game at Sheffield United in April 1992.

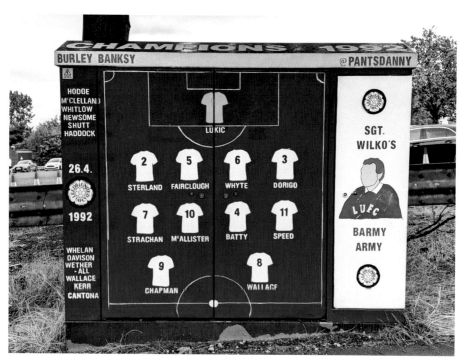

Burley Banksy's street art tribute to Sergeant Wilko's Barmy Army, the 1992 championship side.

A mural of Gary Speed in Bramley, painted by Claire Bentley-Smith, aka Poshfruit Creative, and supported by the Leeds United Supporters' Trust. Speed committed suicide and the mural was created in partnership with Andy's Man Club, a mental health charity.

Bill Fotherby polarised fans' opinions, as demonstrated by this graffiti on a bridge over the River Aire on Whitehall Road, Leeds, 1990s. (© Julian Barker)

Replica Leeds United shirts from the 1980s and 1990s as sold at the club shop at Elland Road.

The 2017 mural at the Lowfields Road subway depicting the championship midfield of Gary Speed, David Batty, Gary McAllister and Gordon Strachan. Howard Wilkinson is shown carrying the trophy. Funded via Crowdfunder by the Leeds United Supporters' Trust, it was painted by local artist Jameson Rogan.

On the side of the Yorkshire Rose pub in Guiseley, Phil Harris' mural commemorates Marcelo Bielsa, Howard Wilkinson and Don Revie with the Championship trophy they won with Leeds.

Caspian chairman Chris Akers in 1996 following the company's purchase of Leeds United.

A shocked Howard Wilkinson after the announcement of his sacking in September 1996.

Painting of Lucas Radebe on the side of Sweeney Todd Barbers on Potternewton Lane. It was painted by Adam Duffield, aka Meds One. It shows Radebe in action against the backdrop of his national South African flag. The phrase 'This is my hero' was used by Nelson Mandela on a visit to Leeds after seeing Radebe in a crowd. Radebe was a regular at the barbers.

Howard Wilkinson in reflective mood around 2015.

Gary Edwards, one of Leeds United's most loyal fans and a celebrated writer, partying during preseason in Finland in 1999. (© Gary Edwards)

In front of the United club shop at Elland Road a plaque commemorates Chris Loftus and Kevin Speight, who were killed in Turkey in 2000 before Leeds' game with Galatasaray.

The author with Steve Hodge pre-game at Elland Road, February 2020.

The author pictured with Tony Dorigo, Steve Hodge, Jon Newsome, Mel Sterland and Chris Whyte in April 2022 at the Cedar Court Hotel, Harrogate, during a tribute evening for the champions of 1992.

Mel Sterland pictured in April 2022 at the Cedar Court Hotel, Harrogate, during a tribute evening for the champions of 1992.

The author pictured with Jon Newsome in April 2022 at the Cedar Court Hotel, Harrogate, during a tribute evening for the champions of 1992.

Carlton Palmer and David O'Leary watch a reserve game at Elland Road in 1994, before departing for a dress dinner with the rest of the first team later that evening. (© Julian Barker)

John Pemberton, Gary McAllister and Carlton Palmer take in a reserve game at Elland Road in 1994. They were off to a black tie dinner with the first team squad that evening. A casual Alan Sutton (in the foreground) passed on that opportunity. (© Julian Barker)

The diggers move in as the club begins work on the redevelopment of the Lowfields Road stand in 1992. (© Julian Barker)

The luckless moment might have convinced Leeds that they would have to settle for a point but suddenly they were gifted a haphazard winner. As Rees came out to meet a Leeds attack, centre-back Bryan Gayle got a dose of the jitters. He seemed unaware of his keeper's advance, saw the ball bounce up off his knee as he tried to see off the danger and then attempted to nod the ball back to Rees. He could only stand in frozen horror as he watched the ball loop over the stricken custodian and on into an unguarded net, his face a mixture of sickly horror and a wry grin. Was he secretly a Leeds fan?

Wilkinson's men had won an extraordinary contest 3-2 and the onus was on Manchester United to match the feat or the championship would be on its way to West Yorkshire. Their nerves betrayed them and they lost 2-0 at Liverpool to confirm Wilkinson's triumph.

The man himself was enjoying a quiet roast lamb dinner at home with Bill Fotherby, Mick Hennigan and their wives.

We were sat having lunch and my son Ben wandered off to watch the television. I said I didn't want to know the result. We were having lunch, we were having a good time, and the result will be the result.

I heard this voice whisper, 'Dad, Liverpool are winning 1-0.' Then a bit later it came again – 'Dad, Liverpool are winning 2-0.' Then the table emptied. I was sat there on my own eating my lunch while they were all in the other room jumping around. I remember there were three minutes to go, then two minutes, then one minute to go ... then within an hour it was chaos outside the house with the media.

The celebrations that followed were equally surreal. ITV had dispatched a camera to Lee Chapman's house where he was watching with Cantona, McAllister and Batty as Leeds' triumph was confirmed.

City Square in Leeds became a focal point for the evening's celebrations with the party carrying on well into the early hours of Monday morning as more and more people descended on the city.

A closing day victory against Norwich was an unnecessary luxury as Leeds hoisted the championship trophy for the third time, eighteen years after the previous triumph.

Wilkinson was the picture of serenity and pride as he savoured his roast lamb and four years of unstoppable success. 'Does it get any better than this?' he thought to himself.

CHAPTER FIFTEEN

Au Revoir

The summer of 1992 was a joyous time to be associated with Leeds United Football Club. The glow of the title triumph persisted for months and Howard Wilkinson was feted as a messiah. He was given free rein to strengthen his squad as he saw fit, as confirmed by Leslie Silver at the club's Annual General Meeting.

'I can assure shareholders that the board will continue our policy of providing the manager with the necessary funds for team strengthening, in order that Leeds United can continue to compete with the best in Europe.'

It was a shock that the money went on Arsenal's David Rocastle (a club record £2 million) and former United starlet Scott Sellars from Blackburn (£800,000) as it was in midfield where Leeds were at their strongest. Concerns about how long Gordon Strachan could maintain his excellent form prompted Wilkinson's dealings. A reparatory operation was planned for Strachan's chronic back problems and at thirty-five he was approaching the end of a spectacular career.

There was no question that the club had the wherewithal to push the boat out. Even after the heavy transfer outlay, there was a pre-tax profit of £509,000, only the second surplus since 1980. United's success in the FA Cup in 1987 had produced a marginal gain of £12,524 but that was an anomaly in more than a decade of living in the red.

Most of the cash for Wilkinson's spending came by way of an £850,000 loan from Leslie Silver and a secured loan of £1.2 million.

The board also found money to start work on the new East Stand, which when completed would be the largest cantilever stand in Europe. The Lowfields Road Stand was demolished and the new stand built over the lower terraced section. The final bill was £5.5 million, with £2 million coming from a grant from the Football Trust. A further contribution was raised via the 'Leeds United Bond', with more than 5,000 supporters paying

£700,000 to buy bonds which would entitle them to discounts on season tickets.

The AGM was held in the club's brand-new banqueting suite, constructed on the back of the West Stand. Its development necessitated the removal of the famous old blue façade which had fronted the stadium ever since the fire and reconstruction of the West Stand in 1957. There were some complaints about what was seen as disrespect for the club's heritage, the move condemned as a corporate chasing of the Yankee dollar.

There was also some disquiet at a critical change behind the scenes. It had long been clear that the Wilko-Silver-Fotherby inner circle ran the show; if it was important, then it was agreed by the trio, end of conversation.

The change was formalised at an Extraordinary General Meeting on 9 December when Fotherby, Silver, and vice-chairman Peter Gilman pushed through the establishment of a holding company that sat above the board. The trio persuaded shareholders to accept a 'simpler, executive shareholding to increase the efficiency of decision-making'. The three men gained absolute control as the holders of executive management shares, freezing out the other directors, whose ranks included Peter Ridsdale.

Ridsdale commented, 'I became nothing more than a glorified season ticket holder. There was nothing improper in this restructuring, but I could not help wondering why it was being done.' Fellow director Maxwell Holmes went even further, resigning his seat in protest at the concentration of power.

The club's financial outlook appeared bright given the increased television fees negotiated by the newly formed Premier League while qualification for the European Cup offered an exciting new challenge.

The players warmed up for the new season by playing in the Makita Tournament, which Elland Road hosted. The fans revelled in the 'in yer face' naked aggression of David Batty as he took on Roberto Mancini and his star-studded Sampdoria team almost single-handed. Batty's sly smirk after one confrontation and refusal to tone it down almost caused a diplomatic incident. Certainly, Mancini threw all his toys out of the pram as the fans bayed their appreciation for their local hero.

While the long-anticipated establishment of the Premier League was the big new thing, it was another, less-celebrated change which had the greater short-term impact for Leeds United and several rival teams. The rules regarding passes back to the goalkeeper had been changed. Previously, keepers had been allowed to pick the ball up, but that was now banned. John Lukic struggled to adjust – riddled by anxiety at having to play only with his feet, Lukic was like a rabbit in the headlights whenever the ball came back to him, his clearances rushed and panicky. The United defenders were also unsettled by the change – Chris Fairclough and, more particularly, Chris Whyte had often relied on a ball back to Lukic to get them out of trouble.

The change brought panic to the heart of the defence and it took months to get used to it, undermining the previously sound rearguard.

When Lukic and co. kicked off the season proper with the Charity Shield curtain-raiser against Liverpool, everyone was waiting to see how the Leeds keeper and Liverpool counterpart Bruce Grobbelaar would cope with the new rule.

They didn't have long to wait. As the ball came back to him early on, Lukic showed his self-doubt, slicing wildly into the stands. Television pundit Andy Gray, a fierce critic of the change, sneered, 'I just think that is the perfect example regarding it … Is that making the game any better, when you see the goalkeeper under pressure like that, just lumping the ball out of play? I don't think so.'

The day was better remembered, though, for an exciting match, settled by a United man on peak form. Eric Cantona never played a better game for Leeds, netting an extraordinary hat-trick to secure a 4-3 victory.

His first was a thumping right-foot drive between two defenders from near the penalty spot; the second came when Cantona nodded a McAllister free kick on to Wallace before lashing the knock-down past Grobbelaar; and the third came from a deft header as the Frenchman soared above Mark Wright to steer the ball gently into the net. The cries of 'Ooh, aah, Cantona!' from adoring Leeds fans rang round Wembley. It was a magnificent opening.

Leeds began the inaugural Premier League campaign promisingly – two Lee Chapman goals were enough to beat Wimbledon at Elland Road and they returned from Villa Park with a laudable draw.

They were shaken out of any complacency with a sobering 4-1 defeat at Middlesbrough, the country's supposed best midfield overrun and a brittle defence found badly wanting.

'I had a feeling this morning, and again before the match, that something wasn't quite right,' said Wilkinson. 'Perhaps it was something they ate. We were well turned over by a better team, they headed better, tackled better, passed better, finished better. You name it, we didn't do it, you name it, they did do it. All credit to them.'

Insisting it was too early to draw conclusions about the season ahead, Wilkinson said he would make the players watch the video to learn from their mistakes.

He declined to make changes, trusting the men that had won the title. His instincts were spot on – Leeds hammered Tottenham 5-0 with Cantona contributing another hat-trick.

Determined to right the wrongs of Ayresome Park, Leeds were at Tottenham's throats from the off. Spurs keeper Erik Thorsvedt was as apprehensive about the new back pass rule as Lukic and he sliced an early ball behind in front of the Kop. Leeds went close from the corner and Cantona's overhead kick from another corner had the home crowd on their feet.

With no one quite sure how, the game reached twenty minutes without a goal. Then, suddenly, Tottenham's world collapsed.

Cantona played a one-two with Batty but lost possession and the ball ran wide. Thorsvedt attempted to prevent the corner, but only succeeded in setting up Wallace, who found the empty net from a tight angle.

Spurs were soon three in arrears with Cantona volleying home and then heading in his second. Early in the second half he completed his hat-trick after the ball ran loose from a Chapman header.

The pair combined again midway through the second half, Cantona laying the ball square for Chapman to fire home with Thorsvedt completely out of position after failing to collect Batty's through ball.

Post-match, Wilkinson beamed, 'In the last four seasons we have come back like this every time we have been beaten. There was not much wrong on Saturday, and the same players deserved the chance to rectify matters.'

The result reassured supporters that all was right with the world, but they would have a rude awakening. Leeds continued to stutter with draws at home to Liverpool and away to Oldham before slumping to defeat at Manchester United. It was apparent that all was not well in the camp, and despite the continuing adulation from the fans for Cantona, his relationship was poor with both Chapman and Wilkinson.

Wilkinson said of the Frenchman, 'Eric likes to do what he likes when he likes – and then f***s off. We'd all want a bit of that.' Not surprisingly, Cantona saw it differently and pushed the blame back onto Wilkinson, claiming that he did not like strong personalities and that he was jealous of the rapport Cantona enjoyed with the fans.

The Frenchman's contribution to Leeds' European Cup return brought evidence for and against Wilkinson's claim. United were thrashed 3-0 at Stuttgart in the first leg, though Cantona showed moments of brilliance. His chip had the goalkeeper floundering and then his header found the woodwork. But the Germans overpowered Leeds thereafter and hopes of a money-spinning run appeared over.

Elland Road witnessed an extraordinary comeback in the second leg, Cantona outdoing himself with a wonderful performance on an epic evening.

No British side had ever come back from a three-goal deficit in Europe and the task was labelled 'Mission Impossible'. The fans agreed and the crowd barely topped 20,000.

From somewhere, Leeds recovered all their championship-winning spirit and forced Stuttgart onto the defensive. Speed's volleyed first goal set the spirits racing but when Stuttgart equalised, the away goal meant that Leeds needed five to get through.

McAllister's penalty sent Leeds into the break ahead on the night and inspired a second-half siege. Goals from Cantona and Chapman hinted that the miracle might yet be on, but somehow Stuttgart stumbled through the final ten minutes without further damage.

The 4-1 outcome put Leeds out on the away goals rule, but a replay was ordered when it was discovered that the German side had fielded too many foreign players in the match. Leeds won the replayed tie 2-1 on a night of high drama in Barcelona's Camp Nou. It was the prose of Carl Shutt rather than the poetry of Cantona that was decisive on the night, the Frenchman barely figuring. The result lifted the spirits of a side which had yet to win away in the Premier League and were bumbling along in mid-table.

The fillip was short-lived. Leeds lost both legs of their second-round tie 'Battle of Britain' against Rangers and a 4-0 hammering by Manchester City left them thirteenth. They crashed out of the League Cup at Watford in what turned out to be Cantona's final game for the club. He had scored eleven goals in twenty matches, but the schism between Cantona and Wilkinson was dangerously deep.

When the Frenchman was taken off after a disappointing performance against Rangers at Ibrox, he stormed straight down the tunnel, and Wilkinson dropped him for the next match at QPR.

'Rangers was the start of his downfall,' recalled Jon Newsome. 'History has shown that Eric was a very headstrong individual, and under Howard Wilkinson you all had your own roles to play on the field. If you didn't do what he asked you to do, it was quite simple, he'd get someone else to do it and you wouldn't be playing. Eric wanted to do things his own way.'

'There were problems,' said Cantona. 'One moment he would tell me that he wants me to know that I owe everything to him, that I am only a Frenchman lost in the English league and at other times he would say to me that without me the team is nothing and that I am the essential part. "You put him in the shade," Leeds supporters told me after my departure. I can't believe that this was the reason. However, it became more and more clear that he wanted to get rid of me.'

There were rumours that Cantona was having an affair with Chapman's actress wife, Lesley Ash. Whether or not there was any substance to the stories, Wilkinson clearly felt that the Frenchman was a disruptive influence on the team spirit which he valued so highly – Cantona had become bigger than the club.

'Eric had made up his mind that he couldn't relate to big Lee Chapman as a player,' said Gordon Strachan.

He found it hard to understand how Chappy played and Chappy found it difficult to understand him. We had to play a different style ... We didn't have megabucks to change the whole side just to suit Eric

Cantona ... Eric just couldn't understand what we were at. It frustrated him, there's no doubt about that.

When we went to Rangers, he just didn't produce a performance. There were a lot of places he didn't produce. We needed a bit of help ... We needed to be met a wee bit. It might have bought some time for him to meet us, and we might have been able to bring in some better players to play with him. He had just made up his mind he wanted to leave; there was no way he wanted to stay.

The issue was resolved by a chance telephone call by Bill Fotherby. He rang Manchester United to ask whether full-back Denis Irwin might be available for transfer back to the club where he had started his career.

Red Devils chairman Martin Edwards said there was no chance, but Fotherby nagged him to check with Alex Ferguson.

As expected, Ferguson rejected the request, but when Edwards asked him, 'Would you take Cantona if I could get him?' Ferguson replied, 'Too bloody right I would!'

When Fotherby rang back, Edwards told him Fergie wasn't interested but would take Cantona off Leeds' hands, almost as if they were doing them a favour.

Fotherby admitted, 'We're open to selling him, but we have one problem at our end. He's very popular. The crowd love him. We'll get slaughtered. Howard will do it, but only if we do it very quickly.'

Edwards: 'What do you want for him?'
Fotherby: '£1.6 million.'
Edwards: 'I won't pay that. But we'll take him off your hands for a million.'
Fotherby: 'I can't do a million! I told you I'd get slaughtered. I'd get lynched at that price. I can't go any lower than £1.2 million.'
Edwards: 'Bill, I'll give you a million.'
Fotherby: 'Well, can I say it's £1.2 million?'
Edwards: 'You can say what you like.'

On 26 November, the Frenchman became a Manchester United player for a bargain basement fee. The move left Cantona branded a traitor by the Leeds faithful and had grave repercussions for Wilkinson, leading to questions regarding his competence. It was one of several questionable transfer dealings over the next four years. One such saw Scott Sellars depart for Newcastle before the end of March, leaving Leeds with a loss of £100,000 on a deal that lasted barely nine months and yielded just six starts. Rocastle did slightly better with eleven starts in a patchy season spent as an expensive deputy for Gordon Strachan.

Without Cantona, Leeds looked good in beating Arsenal 3-0, but then lost to Chelsea and Forest and slipped down to fifteenth, heralding a difficult winter.

Form was patchy, particularly on the road where they could return not a single victory all season. Only the presence of even poorer sides and decent home results kept Leeds in with a chance of staying up. A 5-2 victory against Blackburn in April was an utter aberration, yet Wilkinson had sufficient confidence to blood a clutch of teenagers in the closing weeks. Rob Bowman, Mark Tinkler, Jamie Forrester, Kevin Sharp and Noel Whelan were all summoned from the side that would beat Manchester United to lift the FA Youth Cup.

Despite the unflappable face Wilkinson showed to the world, Leeds finished a scant two points clear of relegation after a single win from their final ten games. It was one of the worst title defences in history.

The optimism of 1992 had been rudely snuffed out.

CHAPTER SIXTEEN

Recovery

'I'd like to make Leeds United a winning team again and if that means changes, then changes there'll be ... Hopefully, maybe some of the kids will come pushing through, hopefully, we'll bring in extra players, quality players and inevitably, as is football, that may mean some people going out.'

Howard Wilkinson was as aware as anyone of how the departure of Eric Cantona had damaged his standing with the fans and called into question his understanding of the transfer market. He also fully appreciated that after such a dismal attempt to retain their league title he had to do something to get the side back on track. There was plenty of promise in the youth ranks, but they needed time to mature and that meant Wilkinson had to turn to the market.

Unconvinced that thirty-two-year-old Lee Chapman could still deliver the goals needed, Wilkinson's priority was a new striker. He set his sights on Duncan Ferguson, the towering Dundee United hit man.

Wilkinson had brought in the young Norwegian Frank Strandli, but it was clear that he was not yet ready for the Premier League and the manager badly needed someone who could hit the ground running.

Twenty-one-year-old Ferguson had already won a Scotland cap and made waves north of the border. Wilko was given permission to push the boat out and tabled an offer of £3.25 million, which would have smashed the club record set when bringing in David Rocastle the previous summer. A deal was as good as done, with Dundee United vice-chairman Doug Smith telling the press, 'Terms have been agreed between ourselves and Leeds and as far as we are concerned it is between Leeds and Ferguson.'

There was an impasse, however, when Fotherby began negotiating personal terms with Ferguson and he opted to stay instead in Scotland, moving to Rangers for a British record fee of £4 million.

The protracted negotiations left little time to sort out an alternative. Wilko's contingency plan was a move closer to home, bringing in Sheffield United striker Brian Deane for £2.7 million.

Another newcomer at preseason training was thirty-five-year-old centre-back David O'Leary, signed on a free transfer when Arsenal manager George Graham declared him past his best after two decades at Highbury.

Wilkinson also oversaw the departure of a number of players, with old stager Mervyn Day one of the first. Carl Shutt and Chris Whyte quickly followed, both off to Birmingham. Chapman took the opportunity of a fresh start at Portsmouth in early August.

Also leaving was right-back David Kerslake, who had only arrived in March in a £500,000 deal to cover for Mel Sterland's injury. An injury at Anfield in his eighth appearance ended his season. Wilkinson asked nineteen-year-old Irish forward Gary Kelly to try his hand at full-back and he seized the opportunity, impressing with his pace and energy down the right flank. He looked as if he was born to play there.

O'Leary showed his undoubted class in the first game of the new season, partnering Chris Fairclough in a 1-1 draw at Manchester City, with fellow debutant Brian Deane getting the Leeds goal.

Leeds, sporting their new away kit of blue and yellow stripes, should have won the game easily but were frustrated by an inspired display from City keeper Tony Coton. They dominated the game but wasted a hatful of chances, with the match appearing certain to finish goalless until the last three minutes.

City had rarely got a sight of John Lukic's goal but a cross from the left found an unmarked Mike Sheron deep in the area as United's concentration deserted them. Lukic performed wonders to block Sheron's instant strike, but Garry Flitcroft fired home from the loose ball. It was a real kick in the teeth after such a dominating display.

Leeds were not ready to concede, however, and Deane thought he had equalised when he slid the ball in after a mix-up in the City defence. Referee Dermot Gallagher awarded a free kick for a supposed foul on Coton. Undeterred, Leeds came again and forced a corner as the game ran into injury-time. Gary Speed met the corner kick from Gary McAllister but Coton got to his header. Deane gleefully slammed home the loose ball to snatch a point.

Leeds had performed well and Wilkinson went with the same starting XI three days later for the game with West Ham, sticking with Kelly and eighteen-year-old Leeds-born striker Noel Whelan.

West Ham never came close to making a game of it, but Leeds struggled to get a shot on target in a scrappy contest. United scored the game's only goal as the game moved into the last half-hour, after a persistent Deane bored his way towards goal from the right flank. He shook off Hammers challenges and seemed ready to profit but Gary Speed intervened with a well-placed finish into the bottom corner.

'I was just about to nick the ball past the keeper,' joked Deane, though everyone knew he would have probably ballooned any shot high and wide.

Hopes of a decent season were quickly deflated – Norwich won 4-0 at Elland Road and O'Leary limped out of the game with an injury that kept him out of the reckoning for six months. Defeats followed at Arsenal and Liverpool and Leeds plummeted to eighteenth in the early table.

When asked if the injury to O'Leary would lead to a change of strategy, Wilkinson responded, 'Well, to a degree it did because one of the reasons I brought David here was to give us, give the younger players the benefit of his experience, particularly the young defenders, and particularly the young central defenders, Newsome and David Wetherall. And I think despite his injury we've seen some of the benefits of that. I think, had he not got injured, we'd have seen even more benefits from it, but I think we have seen benefits. I think, for instance, he's helped young David Wetherall a lot and he's a player who I think from the start of the season has changed dramatically. He now looks like a footballer.'

After conceding eight goals in three games, John Lukic forfeited his place to Mark Beeney.

Wilko: 'I don't think you can lay the blame at one person. I think people make mistakes, sometimes as a result of those mistakes you lose games, those mistakes contribute to you losing games. He'd played the whole of the season before, we'd had a summer off and I thought he started the season in similar vein to that which he'd finished the last. So, I didn't think he was performing as well as he could. I thought that was having an effect on other people and I decided that the best solution was to have a change, a, to give him a chance to sit back and take stock, b, if it was necessary to shake him up and c, to give the young boy, who'd worked very, very hard since he arrived, a chance in the Premier League.'

Gordon Strachan smacked home a beauty in the next game to see off Oldham and confidence was restored with five league victories on the bounce. That run included United's first away victory since their title season, against Southampton at The Dell.

Leeds were third by the beginning of October and the famous championship midfield was still functioning as well as ever, despite concerns about Strachan's age. Surprisingly, the first of the four to fall by the wayside was David Batty, off in a shock £2.75 million move in October to join big-spending Jack Walker's revolution at Blackburn.

Wilko: 'The people who are experts on the money side said that the sort of money we were getting for David Batty was at that time essential to the well-being, the long-term well-being of this football club. I listen to what they say, I understand their reasons for saying it and at the end of the day I have to go along with better-informed opinion than my own as to what is best in a particular area at which I am not, and don't claim to be, an expert.'

Despite the loss of Batty, results continued to be positive and Leeds were up to second in the table by the end of November, though a massive fourteen points in the wake of runaway leaders Manchester United.

The performance of the season came in a 4-1 hammering of Chelsea with some spectacular finishes from Deane (his first at Elland Road), Wallace (two) and Rocastle – it was possibly the finest game of Rocastle's time at Elland Road.

An inability to finish games off was the fly in Wilkinson's ointment. A draw at Everton on 23 November was the fourth in five games, but Leeds smashed the sequence with three straight victories, each featuring a goal from the impressive Wallace. He had netted nine goals from his sixteen Premier League appearances. He kept the run going in the following game at Norwich, but it wasn't enough with goals from Chris Sutton and Efan Ekoku ending an unbeaten run of fourteen in the league. Leeds should have won – they hit the post and dominated the contest. 'You can analyse and scrutinise but at the end of the day what made the difference was luck, we didn't have it and Norwich did,' said a rueful Wilkinson.

Rocastle was a member of the side that beat his old club Arsenal the week before Christmas, but just as he seemed finally set to make a mark at Elland Road, Wilkinson sprang something of a surprise. Rocastle left in a straight swap deal for Manchester City's England wide man David White, both players valued at £2 million. Wilkinson had finally decided to call time on a player who had never found a niche, starting just seventeen games in his eighteen months at the club. He claimed that when he first brought in Rocastle he was a like-for-like long-term replacement for Strachan, but 'White gives me something different.' All parties thought they were benefiting from the deal and Rocastle was an instant hit with the City fans.

City manager Brian Horton told the press, 'Sometimes, you have to lose a bit to gain a bit and I think we have gained here.'

Rocastle described his time at Leeds as a 'bad experience' and welcomed the chance 'to show I can still play. People ask me why I was not in the team and I honestly could not answer. Through no fault of my own I was not able to play.'

White was a regular starter for the rest of the season, but it was April before his first Premier League goal, against QPR. He quickly added a second in the 4-0 victory that saw Leeds retain the fifth place they would hold to the end of the campaign.

White scored in each of the final three games and Leeds signed off with a 5-0 rout of relegated Swindon Town on their own ground. The result meant the Wiltshire club conceded 100 for the season and United's final position saw them receive place money of £700,500.

Deane opened the scoring after seventeen minutes, running in to sidefoot home a hooked delivery from Wallace. Eleven minutes later, White notched his fifth goal in seven matches from a Gary Kelly cross. Whelan came on for White in the second half after the latter injured his ankle and Leeds continued to dominate, Wallace, Deane and Fairclough rubbing in the advantage.

'The players' attitude was first-class,' said Wilkinson. 'So was the quality of our play and the goals we scored were excellent.'

It was a season that ultimately brought only disappointment despite some breathtaking performances. The defeat of Swindon was only United's fifth on the road; if their form on their travels had only matched their strong home record, they might have challenged for the title. But Wilkinson appeared to have got his men back on track.

CHAPTER SEVENTEEN

Rebuilding

The summer of 1994 caught Leeds United in a crucial period of transition. They had recovered much of the ground they lost in their post-title season and new signing Brian Deane had effectively replaced Lee Chapman. Deane was not as productive in front of goal as Chapman and could often frustrate with his clumsiness and haphazard shooting, but he certainly provided a focal point up front.

Fifth place and some decent football warmed the heart but Howard Wilkinson was not fooled. David Batty had gone, Gordon Strachan's influence was waning and Mel Sterland had been forced into retirement through injury. Of his title-winning squad, only Lukic, Dorigo, Fairclough, McAllister, Wallace and Speed were still active members of the first team. Gary Kelly had brought youthful energy and verve to the right flank, but Wilkinson was patently aware that he needed to strengthen. Unfortunately, his summer foray into the market was a bit of a damp squib.

There were few protests when he got rid of fringe players Frank Strandli and Ray Wallace. Even the departure of Jon Newsome caused little consternation, the £1 million received from Norwich representing decent value.

Wilkinson returned to former club Sheffield Wednesday to sign ungainly England midfielder Carlton Palmer for £2.6 million and full-back Nigel Worthington for £325,000, bemusing many and infuriating some who dismissed both men as substandard. How could anyone seriously see Palmer as an upgrade on Batty? Palmer and Worthington would be lasting symbols of Leeds' mid-1990s malaise under Wilkinson, underwhelming performers who represented a retrograde step rather than any advance.

The manager also signed two unknown South Africans, striker Phil 'Chippa' Masinga, who opted for Leeds rather than Bobby Robson's Sporting Lisbon, and defender Lucas Radebe, for a combined fee of just over

£500,000. The price was a bargain, but the initial reaction from the fans was tepid.

They had been wound up to expect more, with the identified target the Czech international striker Tomas Skuhravy. Indeed, a £3 million fee was agreed with Genoa for a player whose five goals in the 1990 World Cup finals had made him the second highest scorer at the tournament.

The deal came so close to fruition that the media were invited to a press conference and Jurgen Klinsmann had been lined up to replace Skuhravy at Genoa.

When Skuhravy was quoted by a Czech news agency as saying, 'The offer was not what I had expected,' Bill Fotherby dismissed speculation that Leeds hadn't been prepared to satisfy Skuhravy's ambitions and claimed he was talking about his contract at Genoa. However, Skuhravy rejected the move to Leeds at the eleventh hour, citing his wife's dislike of shops in Leeds as his reason, but the pretence fooled nobody.

Whatever the reality of matters, disgruntled supporters wrote the entire affair off as another insubstantial flight of fancy by Fotherby.

Luckily, Masinga was an instant success, scoring freely in preseason. Radebe's introduction was less smooth, completion of his signing held up by a delay over his work permit. Even after completing the deal, his introduction to the first team was held back by a series of injuries.

Palmer and Worthington made their debuts on the opening day at West Ham, while Masinga came off the bench three minutes before the end of the goalless draw. He was in the starting XI three days later when Leeds beat Arsenal courtesy of a goal from nineteen-year-old Leeds-born striker Noel Whelan. His curling last-minute effort from distance was hopelessly misjudged by England keeper David Seaman.

Masinga scored after three minutes of the following game, at home to Chelsea, and Whelan made it 2-0 after eighteen minutes but the Londoners fought back to secure a 3-2 victory.

Whelan scored again to settle the subsequent game against Crystal Palace and he and Masinga were on duty once more when Leeds faced the acid test of their ambitions, at home to Manchester United.

Wetherall gave Leeds a twelfth-minute lead with a bobbling shot from a corner and then Whelan danced through the Manchester defence at the start of the second half to set up Deane's close-range goal. Eric Cantona pulled one back from the penalty spot after a clumsy challenge by Deane on Ince, but Leeds held out for a famous victory, climbing to sixth as a result.

Whelan had been outstanding against the Red Devils and continued to suggest that he was the real thing, his two goals seeing off Manchester City on 1 October. He also scored the winner against Leicester at the end of the month and the only goal when Leeds beat Forest in November. But then he mislaid his scoring boots and began to slip down the pecking order. Leeds had hit a glass ceiling and struggled to get any higher than sixth, always prone to defeat just as they appeared ready to advance. Wilkinson was beside himself with frustration at the team's inability to build any real momentum.

Now Masinga found some decent goal-scoring form, a brace in a 3-1 victory at Arsenal the week before Christmas, a nine-minute hat-trick as Leeds smashed Walsall in the FA Cup, two more in the 4-0 defeat of QPR and the winner against Oldham at the end of January.

But there was a new star in town – Fotherby's trawling of the European leagues finally came good. *Clubcall* headlined with 'Leeds sign African superstar' as Leeds confirmed that they had signed Eintracht Frankfurt striker Tony Yeboah.

The £3.4 million fee set a new club record and was the key deal in net outgoings for the year of £3.3 million. Such a huge burden drove the club into the red with a loss of £2.4 million, the first deficit in four years.

Yeboah's name meant nothing to anyone in England at the time, but he was soon to become hot property. His record of 68 goals in 123 Bundesliga games for Eintracht was impressive, but it was about all anybody knew about the striker. Stories began to seep out about the way he pioneered the cause of the black footballer in Germany, turning the racist monkey noises to cheers with his epic displays. This was a man of some substance, stocky and strong, yet deft of foot and blessed with extraordinary shooting prowess.

Wilkinson used Yeboah sparingly at first, giving him time to acclimatise. His debut came as sub for Masinga after the South African had scored twice against QPR on 24 January and there were more second-half cameos as Masinga made way against Oldham and Blackburn. Yeboah's big moment came in the FA Cup against Manchester United at Old Trafford, brought off the bench at the start of the second half. Within seven minutes, the Ghanaian opened his scoring account for Leeds. It was an untidy goal, the ball bundled in from a yard out after he appeared to have missed it. The goal was rendered worthless by the three scored by the men from Manchester, but Yeboah was suddenly a star. The Leeds fans who surged forward in the stand behind the goal knew as much.

Could he keep it up? You bet! Three days later, Yeboah scored the only goal of the game against Everton, added two-goal hauls at Chelsea and Leicester before notching a vital second goal in the 3-0 defeat of Coventry.

But the best came at the beginning of April, when Leeds faced Ipswich at Elland Road. Within four minutes of kick-off, Yeboah's work had begun, taking McAllister's through ball in his stride, rounding keeper Craig Forrest and rolling the ball home.

Gary Speed made it two just after the half-hour with the fiftieth goal of his Leeds career, but the day was all about Yeboah. He added two more before the break, completing his hat-trick with a cracking shot from inside the box on the stroke of half-time.

The expected second-half onslaught failed to materialise, although Yeboah headed against the woodwork and McAllister and Wallace both had efforts disallowed.

Wilkinson purred with pleasure at the end. 'Perhaps it's too often used, but I thought his finishing was world-class ... His goals and perhaps more importantly his goal threat have given the side that little extra injection of confidence which comes from seeing good work produce something.'

Three more Yeboah goals in an end-of-season nine-match unbeaten run saw Leeds finish fifth and hint that they could make a genuine title tilt the following year. The Ghanaian's haul of twelve goals from twenty appearances had the fans drooling.

Just as one player was becoming a new star, another was coming to the end of a remarkable spell at Leeds United. Thirty-seven-year-old Gordon Strachan, his career extended by his much-publicised diet of seaweed pills and bananas, had become increasingly troubled by back problems and sciatica. He announced in October 1994 that he would retire at the end of the season but within a few weeks he announced he was ready to concentrate on coaching. Within two months, his old Manchester United manager, Ron Atkinson, lured him to Coventry City with the promise that he would be groomed to succeed him at Highfield Road.

That and the increased money constituted an offer that Strachan felt unable to refuse – if only the Leeds board had seen fit to make him similar promises, the entire history of the club might have been different. They were content, however, to allow Strachan to move on to pastures new. His final season with Leeds brought only seven lacklustre performances and a sole victory, but his enthusiasm and nous had been a vital component of Wilkinson's dressing room. McAllister had smoothly assumed the role of captain, but Strachan was still the heart and soul of the club.

Before the end of the season, Strachan was back on the field with Coventry and he went on playing for a further two years. His final appearance came at the age of forty, at the time a record in the Premier League.

During his six years at Elland Road, Strachan had been the on-field general that made Wilkinson's team tick. He had reinvigorated the club and his presence around the place would be sorely missed. All good things must come to an end, but it was sad that the reign of Gordon Strachan should end so abruptly, symbolically ending the connection back to 1992's title triumph.

CHAPTER EIGHTEEN

Raging Bull

Tony Yeboah's start to life at Leeds was impressive, but it was in the autumn of 1995 when he really came good, when he showed himself to be one of the finest strikers in world football. The hammer of Yeboah was a constant feature as the Ghanaian struck again and again, each phenomenal strike seemingly outdoing its predecessor. And for a while his presence suggested that Leeds could challenge for the title.

Yeboah was a raging bull of a striker, boasting the rippling, muscle-bound build of a boxer, thick set and strong as an ox. On his day, he was completely unmanageable for defenders, a beast of a man with unbelievable timing to his shooting – an irresistible force.

We were at it straight from the off when Yeboah scored both goals in a 2-1 victory at West Ham. The first was a routine striker's goal, leaping to head home from a Gary Kelly cross, but the second was sumptuous, Yeboah timing a left-footed boomer perfectly. As the ball bounced in front of him in the area, Yeboah took aim and the ball flew into the net like a rocket, leaving goalkeeper Ludek Miklosko flat-footed. It was a wonderfully clean strike, all to do with timing rather than brute power. 'You won't get a better one than that,' said the commentator, but he was wrong, we would get plenty.

There was *that* goal, the one against Liverpool where Yeboah thundered a spectacular drive past a hapless David James as Elland Road roared its appreciation for one of the finest goals ever seen at the stadium. It was voted the greatest goal in the club's history and widely regarded as one of the best the Premier League had ever seen. Astonishing then that a different Yeboah strike was later voted as the Premier League's Goal of the Season.

It was at the start of the second half that the magic moment came, breaking the deadlock of the first period. Tony Dorigo had come under pressure as he sought to pump the ball forward and his booming long ball looked to be going nowhere. Somehow, Rod Wallace beat his man in the air and nodded the ball on and still there seemed no danger, but Yeboah had other ideas. Thirty yards out, he summed things up in an instant and decided to chance his arm, on his supposedly weaker right foot. His strike was one in a million, the sweetest of efforts, catching the falling ball perfectly. It soared towards David James' goal, hinting momentarily that it might go over, until it arced down purposefully and crashed against the underside of the bar, smacking down against the goal line and then booming back into the roof of the net. James had done his best to get to the ball, but it was struck so powerfully that he didn't have a chance. Elland Road roared its appreciation for a historic moment.

'In that moment, everything just happened,' Yeboah told the *Yorkshire Post*. 'You ask me what was going through my head when I hit the ball and I can't answer. It was just something special, a special moment.'

Yeboah himself rated the goal as his favourite ever. 'Liverpool was the best goal,' he smiled. 'Why do I think that? Because it was live on television and everyone was watching. It surprised people. Also, I grew up as a Liverpool fan and their team had Rush, Barnes, players I admired.'

Yeboah allowed someone else onto the scoresheet in the next game, goals from Gary Speed and David White enough to see off Aston Villa and complete a perfect 100 per cent start for Leeds. They were three points clear of the pack, though a superb Newcastle side passed them on goal difference when they won their game in hand.

It wasn't a one-man show; Leeds were playing superbly in that spell, McAllister and Speed on top form in midfield, Kelly and Dorigo contributing splendidly from full-back, Deane and Palmer ungainly but hard to cope with.

Leeds stumbled to a draw at Southampton and defeat at Tottenham, though Yeboah was in the goals again at White Hart Lane.

Then came another Yeboah wonder show as Leeds began their UEFA Cup campaign away to a star-studded Monaco side.

It took Yeboah only three minutes to get the show on the road. When a curling high ball from Dorigo came soaring into the area, keeper Fabien Piveteau looked to have caught the ball cleanly but spilled it as he crashed into centre-back Lillian Thuram. Yeboah was on it in an instant, throwing himself at the bouncing ball and hooking it adroitly over his head and into the net.

That gave Leeds the perfect platform and they grew effortlessly into the game, Yeboah marking their dominance with a second goal after sixty-five minutes. He took a throw from McAllister on the right, turned inside and muscled his way clear from his man before suddenly unleashing a curling shot that flew into the top corner past a helpless keeper.

He completed his hat-trick with ten minutes remaining, chasing onto a through ball. He got to it before either the keeper or defender Basile Boli and clipped it into the empty net as his two opponents crashed into each other and lay dazed.

'Words cannot describe Tony Yeboah nor his importance to the team,' beamed Howard Wilkinson at the end. 'He's always been able to score straightforward goals, but increasingly he is scoring more difficult ones. That is a great result for us.

Frankly, I have not come across anybody quite like him. He will tell you that if he gets the ball in the box he will score, and he does.'

There was more to his performance than merely a striker at the peak of his form, with Carlton Palmer pulling the curtain on the pair's antics on the eve of the game.

One of the stories was I used to have a drink the night before the game. We've finished dinner … He said, 'Where are you going, C?' I said, 'I'm going up the rooftop bar to have a drink.' So he said, 'I'll come with you.' I said, 'Tony, I don't think that's a good idea, mate. The gaffer knows I have a drink, but I'm not getting involved here.' 'No worries, no worries.'

So I'm having a glass of wine, just sitting there, beautiful views looking over Monaco. We've got a tough game. They've got a good side. They've got Blanc, Deschamps in there, good side. We've got a tough game on our hands tomorrow. He's playing up front on his own.

So, I said to him, you need to get some rest, son. It could be a tough gig tomorrow. So he starts having a brandy. I said to him, 'Tony, I really don't think this is a good idea mate.' He must have had about four large brandies. I said, 'You get yourself to bed and don't say anything to the gaffer.'

The next day he scores a hat-trick. And he's shouting in the dressing room, 'it's the brandy, it's the brandy!'

I'm going, 'Tony, don't say that! The gaffer's going to be at me!'

Palmer has nothing but praise for his former teammate's style in front of goal.

'Tony was brilliant,' he continued. 'Tony was absolutely brilliant. Loved him to death, great, great footballer. He was a phenomenal goalscorer. Anything that was played into him in and around the box, it was like "boom" and it stuck to him.

And he had a big old a***. Once he struck that a*** into you, if you got too tight and he spun you on that left-hand side forget it, because he only used to move the ball half a yard and then it was violent. Everything was violent. But he could play.'

Leeds returned to domestic football with a drab defeat to QPR and a draw against Notts County in the Coca-Cola Cup but then came another big moment in the Yeboah story, a memorable trip to Selhurst Park to face Wimbledon.

Leeds were bang on form, bossing the first half, though it took thirty-nine minutes to make the dominance pay. Palmer came out on top against Peter Fear and then hammered a shot from outside the area into the top corner. It was an impressive effort, but totally eclipsed by what came next as Yeboah launched his one-man destruction of the Dons.

Forty-one minutes and the Ghanaian side-footed home from 6 yards when Deane's cross came in.

Dean Holdsworth had an immediate response with a close-range header from a corner to halve the deficit, but Yeboah was instantly at it again with a phenomenal demonstration of his goalscoring capabilities.

Thirty-five yards out, he chested the ball down after a bout of untidy head tennis, cushioned the ball on his vast left thigh, swerved away from a confronting defender and soared into an impossibly powerful strike from 20 yards. It flew down off the bar and back up into the roof of the net in an eerily similar way to his goal against Liverpool. When Yeboah hit the ball, it always stayed hit.

There was a flowing Leeds move early in the second half when they shipped the ball quickly from man to man in crisp and composed fashion, showing exactly how good they were that autumn. Even Palmer came across as an elegant midfielder in a passage of play that ended with the keeper grateful to tip a curling long-range effort from Gary Kelly over the bar.

Wimbledon snapped back with a second goal, Alan Reeves diving to head home, and the Dons pressed Leeds back for a while, peppering Lukic's goal with some hurry-scurry aggression and long-range shots. United came through the battery unscathed and after seventy-four minutes, Yeboah completed a perfect day for the travelling United fans.

Leeds worked another decent movement to find their way deep into the Wimbledon area and the ball came out to Yeboah on the edge of the box. He controlled it instantly and then despatched it almost casually into the bottom corner.

Leeds successfully completed their task against Monaco despite a 1-0 defeat at Elland Road and then Yeboah was at it again, opening the scoring against Sheffield Wednesday.

McAllister slipped the ball to the striker on the left as if to say, 'Over to you, show them how it's done.' Yeboah turned inside and battered his way through four defenders before slamming the ball into the bottom corner from just outside the area. A second goal from Speed secured the points and Leeds were back up to fourth.

As if sated by his feast, Yeboah went into hibernation, lying fallow for eight games. During that spell Leeds crashed out of the UEFA Cup, blitzed 5-3 at home by PSV and capitulating 3-0 against Arsenal. A hat-trick from McAllister steadied the ship against Coventry and then a Deane goal secured a point at Middlesbrough.

Yeboah was back on the scoresheet against Chelsea a couple of weeks later, the 1-0 victory taking United up from eighth to fifth.

There was a problem looming: the African Cup of Nations was scheduled for January in South Africa. With Yeboah appearing for Ghana and Phil Masinga for South Africa along with Lucas Radebe, United's attacking options would be seriously undermined. Bill Fotherby had been scouting Europe for alternatives for some time with rumours circulating regarding Uruguay's Ruben Sosa, the Macedonian Darko Panchev and Inter wide man Andrei Kanchelskis.

It appeared, however, that Faustino Asprilla was the favoured target. The Parma striker had been a member of the star-studded Colombian side who had gone to the summer's World Cup finals in the United States as dark horses. They demolished Argentina 5-0 in a World Cup qualifier in Buenos Aires in 1993, where Asprilla scored twice. Despite finishing at the bottom of their group in the finals, Asprilla was seen as one of the most exciting strikers in the world. In 1993, he was ranked by FIFA as the sixth-best player in the world.

Fotherby confidently predicted that Asprilla would soon be at Elland Road but the move collapsed after accusations that Asprilla had fired a gun at a wild party at his home. He was under investigation and his movements were restricted.

Fotherby refused to admit defeat and switched his focus to Asprilla's Parma teammate Tomas Brolin. He had come to prominence at Euro 92 when his masterly goal against England put Graham Taylor's team out and took the Swedes through. Brolin finished the tournament as the joint leading scorer. He starred again in the 1994 World Cup finals and was included in the team of the tournament as Sweden finished third.

Fotherby pronounced himself highly delighted with a £4.5 million deal, though Howard Wilkinson appeared less enthusiastic.

The Sun headlined with 'Doubting Tomas' when it was revealed that Brolin had insisted on a get-out clause in his contract which could be exercised the following summer.

Wilkinson: 'It implied a doubt in commitment both on his part and on mine. Buying him when we did meant there was no time to get him properly fit and into the rhythm of the Premiership. I played Brolin too soon, instead of working hard with him for six or seven weeks as I did with Tony Yeboah. Brolin wanted to be in and foolishly I went along with it.'

Nevertheless, on the day of the signing, Wilkinson told the press, 'He is a class player, and I believe he will prove to be an excellent buy for Leeds. I am sure he is going to be an excellent partner for Tony Yeboah.'

Yeboah agreed, saying, 'I am sure Tomas and I are going to work well together. He is truly world-class. He can weigh in with goals of his own and link up with the other players in the side. We are going to be very difficult to defend against.'

Brolin had high hopes. 'Give me a month to get my full fitness back, and to adapt to playing in England, and then I will show people what I can really do. I believe I can help Leeds win the championship again. I have had great support from the fans and gradually regained my fitness. I am really excited about the future at Elland Road.'

Wilkinson told Brolin that he wanted him to play in midfield, the role that the Swede preferred. It was that suggestion which swung the move to Leeds but it never worked out that way and Brolin was generally used up front.

He made his debut as an eighty-second-minute substitute in a 2-1 defeat at Newcastle and got his first start in a League Cup victory against Blackburn. His first goal came in a disastrous 6-2 defeat at Sheffield Wednesday in the week before Christmas. It was an utterly bizarre moment, the goal coming when a Wednesday defender's clearance hit him full in the face before bouncing back over the line.

Wilkinson persisted with the Swede in the side when Leeds hosted Manchester United on Christmas Eve, though Deane and Yeboah were the main strikers.

Wilkinson's men started brightly, opening the scoring after seven minutes from the penalty spot after Nicky Butt handled from a corner. Gary McAllister coolly stroked the ball into the top corner after the storm of Manchester protests.

Deane chipped the ball onto the bar shortly afterwards but then Andy Cole equalised.

Back came Leeds after thirty-seven minutes through Yeboah. He picked up the ball just inside the Manchester half after it ran loose from Paul Parker and stormed through the Red Devils' gaping defence. As he reached the edge of the area, he steadied himself and clipped the ball past Peter Schmeichel for his tenth goal of the campaign.

A Deane header from a chipped Brolin cross in the second half wrapped up a wonderful 3-1 victory.

Brolin scored when Leeds beat Bolton but was dropped for the FA Cup match with Derby a couple of weeks later, with Wilkinson demanding he worked harder on his contribution to the side's defensive efforts. On the eve of taking the flight to South Africa, Yeboah signed off with the fourth goal in an emphatic 4-2 victory.

Wilkinson desperately needed cover for his absentee strikers but he surprised the football world with his choice. Old warrior Lee Chapman returned to Elland Road on a short-term loan from Ipswich. 'We find ourselves in a situation where we are down to the bare bones in terms of strikers,' said Wilkinson. 'I know if I call on him, he will not let me down.'

Chapman had only played twice for Ipswich all season but duly led the line against West Ham the following week. Brolin scored both goals in the 2-0 victory, with Chapman playing a big part in the first. Minutes later, though, Chapman was sent off for elbowing a Hammers defender in an aerial clash.

His suspension did not begin until after the following week's clash at Liverpool and Chapman retained his place. It was an extraordinary day, one which saw all the earlier progress collapse, setting the tone for the remainder of the season.

When Wilkinson ordered Brolin to play up and down the right flank, the Swede saw red, deciding, 'I was going to be piss-poor.' Leeds lost 5-0 and

Chapman was subbed off, returning immediately to Ipswich. Brolin's card was marked as far as Wilko was concerned.

After defeat at Forest, the Swede was dropped for the Premier League match against Aston Villa. 'If Brolin had done well, he would have played,' said Wilkinson. 'I picked a team from fifteen available players ... I decided the team at Villa would be better without Tomas Brolin. If he had been playing brilliantly, I would have picked him – but before we played Liverpool, Brolin was concerned about the amount of defending he had to do for the side. He suggested I reconsider, he expressed the opinion he wasn't very good at it and he felt my decision to leave him out at Villa was eminently sensible.'

Nine players were missing at Villa Park, including five under suspension, and the side was badly depleted – seventeen-year-old Alan Maybury made his debut and the side included second stringers in Rob Bowman and Andy Couzens.

If Brolin was nowhere to be seen, after the game he certainly made himself heard. 'I don't know whether I will be staying with Leeds,' he said, seventy-nine days after arriving. 'I do know what I'm capable of on the soccer field, and I always believe I should be picked in the side. It was very disappointing to be left out. I can't tell if I'm being blamed for recent poor results, but unless the manager selects me, I cannot contribute anything.'

With Leeds completely out of contention in the Premier League, everything rested on the cup competitions. They were looking good in both, making their way to the final of the Coca-Cola Cup and the sixth round in the FA Cup, where they faced Liverpool at Elland Road.

Yeboah had returned from Africa in decent form – he netted three times in seven games, including one in the Coca-Cola semi-final defeat of Birmingham – but Wilkinson went for safety first against Liverpool. He inexplicably opted to contain the Merseysiders rather than going for it, the game ending in the goalless draw that he had apparently sought.

'There isn't anything in my contract to say we must look good on television. I felt our best chance was to keep things tight and try to expose the flaws we had spotted. It didn't work out.' Responding sarcastically to Jimmy Hill's criticism of his team, Wilkinson sneered, 'Yeah, I said to them at half-time you've got to make this more entertaining. Go out and put in an own goal, then two of you lie down, let Liverpool go three-up and everyone can go home happy saying they'd been entertained!'

Leeds lost the Anfield replay 3-0.

Wembley was to provide just as dispiriting a scenario, with Yeboah and Brolin both betraying their misgivings in the days before the Coca-Cola Cup final against Aston Villa. They each indicated that they would seriously consider their long-term future in English football should Leeds fail to win.

Both were keen to play in European competition, and with the tournament Leeds' only remaining route, success was imperative.

'If Leeds are not in Europe, then it will be a very, very difficult situation for me,' admitted Yeboah. 'I will retire in two or three years' time, and I need to be playing at the very top until then. I would have to consider my position carefully, because it is very important for me to be playing in European competition.'

Brolin echoed those views. 'I will speak about my future after the last game of the season, but it is fair to say that it would be easier for me to say yes to staying if Leeds qualify for Europe. Every player wants to play in Europe; it is an important influence.'

During that spring, Wilkinson had become fixated on a 3-5-2 formation as the means of getting the best out of the players at his disposal. Yeboah was a shoo-in for one of the striking roles, but the manager shocked everybody with the choice of the Ghanaian's partner at Wembley. Naming Brolin and Deane on the bench and leaving Masinga and Wallace in the stands, Wilkinson opted for eighteen-year-old Andy Gray, son of Frank and nephew of Eddie.

Bizarrely, Gray was United's stand-out performer on the day, betraying no hint of nerves. He had few competitors; none of his colleagues gave more than a cursory nod at a performance. There was only one side in it, Villa dishing out a 3-0 hammering.

Boos rang down from the Leeds fans at the finish, drowning out the cheers of Villa supporters. They made clear their dissatisfaction with Wilkinson, accusing him of losing the plot. He said later, 'It was more than just them showing their disappointment. It was all very personal ... I was gutted. I couldn't believe the way some of our players performed. I almost wished that one of them would take a swing at the referee or they would start fighting among themselves. Anything to show they were actually interested. What should have been a marvellous experience, win or lose, turned into a nightmare. I was emotionally disembowelled, close to walking away from it all.'

Carlton Palmer pilloried his teammates. 'The lack of effort shown by professional players in as big a game as a League Cup final was nothing short of disgraceful. I didn't play well but at least I tried.'

Brolin came on as a late sub but wasn't happy. 'If I cannot play from the start in a final like that, I have to think about my future. I don't know where my future lies now. I wanted to play on Sunday, but the manager thinks his way and I think mine. Perhaps we should go our separate ways. I have to go away and think about my future and whether I want to play for Leeds. The way I feel at the moment, I think I must try to find another team.'

With a growing feeling that Wilkinson's time had come to an end, Leeds slipped to a thirteenth-place finish. It was a downbeat conclusion to a season that had hinted at so much more with its sparkling opening weeks.

CHAPTER NINETEEN

Caspian: The Root of All Evil

The first football club to go public was Tottenham Hotspur, way back in 1982, but by the mid-1990s, the plc model was almost de rigueur. By May 1999, twenty-one clubs had been listed on the London Stock Exchange, with the money pouring into the game courtesy of BSkyB making football an attractive business.

In 1996, Leeds United were ready to climb aboard the bandwagon. Bill Fotherby had long agitated for a sale, telling Leslie Silver, 'Everyone is doing it, Spurs, Manchester United, Newcastle ... We can't afford to miss the boat.'

Silver had previously been reticent, but his thoughts had turned to retirement and cashing in his chips. He was seventy-one, the league title had been won, Leeds were top-five regulars and the time seemed right. If he was still undecided, any doubts evaporated following a traumatic experience in his own home. Three masked and armed men broke into his house in Leeds on 11 March and bound and gagged him and wife Sheila before stealing jewellery. He suffered with heart problems and finally decided enough was enough.

With Peter Gilman, the third holder of the controlling management shares, equally open to the idea of a sale, the decision was a formality and the board asked financial advisers Rothschilds to gauge the strength of market interest in Leeds United as a business proposition.

English football was overflowing with cash following the establishment of the Premier League and the lucrative television broadcasting deals that came with it. By 1996, silly money was involved and the BSkyB deal boosted United's income by almost £2 million.

The club was now generating significant revenue through its commercial activities and two major sponsorship agreements were the icing on a very rich cake. A deal with Packard Bell provided for advertising on the team strip, at the ground and in the matchday programme. The club also negotiated a contract with Puma for the exclusive right to supply, manufacture, and distribute United's kit. These two agreements catapulted Leeds into the big league for sponsorship.

The club raked in cash from the sale of replica kits and other merchandise in club shops based at the stadium and in Leeds and Wakefield city centres. To ensure that they maximised the rewards from such ventures, the board appointed a director of retailing. Adam Pearson, who had previously worked for Marks & Spencer plc and William Baird plc, took responsibility for exploiting Leeds' commercial potential.

Silver, Fotherby and Gilman might have been unanimous regarding the desire to sell up but could not come to an agreement on which of several offers represented the best option.

There were two main bidders: Conrad plc, a Manchester-based leisure group which numbered Bobby Charlton's consultancy business among its subsidiaries, and Caspian Group, a small media rights company based in London. Caspian, principally involved in the development, production and exploitation of intellectual property rights in children's television, had decided to diversify into sport and former QPR chairman Richard Thompson had joined its board to identify suitable targets.

In June, Caspian tabled an offer which would pay Silver, Fotherby and Gilman £5.5 million apiece, clear the £10 million debt and provide a transfer kitty of £12 million. Their package was to be funded by means of a public share issue, but that seemed a sound proposition with financial advisers confident that £28 million could be raised.

Fotherby and Silver were captivated by the Caspian offer, but Gilman was less enamoured. He favoured the Conrad bid, which was more generous than Caspian's, but Silver and Fotherby were not for turning.

On 4 July, the boards of Caspian and Leeds United announced the terms of a recommended offer and Wilkinson started spending immediately, making Charlton midfielder Lee Bowyer Britain's most expensive teenager in a £2.6 million deal. He had already persuaded Liverpool striker Ian Rush to move to Elland Road on a free transfer and the moves signalled a major programme of team rebuilding.

Caspian's purchase of the shares owned by Fotherby and Silver would give it 65.2 per cent of United's share capital. This obliged Caspian to extend the offer to all other shareholders for fourteen days after the acquisition became unconditional, with the deal to be confirmed at an Extraordinary General Meeting of Caspian shareholders on 31 July.

Gilman claimed that the Caspian offer 'stinks for the fans and under-values the club'. He argued that Fotherby and Silver had breached a gentlemen's agreement that any sale had to be unanimously approved.

So angry was Gilman at what he regarded as betrayal, that he immediately launched a High Court injunction to halt the deal. His goal was to force

Fotherby and Silver to sell their shares to him, allowing him to seal a deal with Conrad. The legal action put a temporary halt to any further transfer activity. Despite having £12 million burning a hole in his pocket, the injunction left Wilkinson sitting on his hands for almost a month.

He cut a frustrated figure, complaining that signing new players was all but impossible after clubs had commenced with their preseason plans. While he had been twiddling his thumbs, his Premier League rivals had been snapping up all the talent on the market. By the time the impasse was broken, he feared that all that would be left were the players that no one else wanted.

While he waited, Phil Masinga, John Lukic, Nigel Worthington and, most regrettably, Gary Speed and Gary McAllister all departed Elland Road. Speed's move was anticipated, but McAllister dealt a grievous blow to Wilkinson when he lost patience with the delayed takeover and threw his lot in with Gordon Strachan at Coventry.

Wilkinson blamed the power struggle for McAllister's departure. He felt the club's uncertain future pushed McAllister into handing in the transfer request that opened the way for Coventry.

'These are difficult times,' said Wilkinson, obviously disappointed that he was unable to persuade McAllister that his future would be best served by staying at Elland Road.

Only a week earlier, McAllister had declared that he would remain at Elland Road for as long as the club wanted him, and he was just a few months into a new three-year contract. However, he became disillusioned as Wilkinson's plans were neutered by the power struggle.

Rod Wallace and the injured Tony Dorigo were thus left as sole survivors from 1992's championship-winning side.

Wilkinson had been clear ever since the League Cup final debacle in the spring that he needed to make big changes. He went into the new season in frustrated mood, knowing that Brolin and Yeboah would be unavailable through injury. When the courts ruled that Fotherby and Silver could complete the sale to Caspian, Wilkinson made two further signings, moving for Crystal Palace keeper Nigel Martyn and Manchester United winger Lee Sharpe, signed for a club record £4.5 million.

'A lot of the off-the-field things I wanted to achieve have been achieved,' said Wilkinson, 'but not all of them. If I could wave a magic wand this afternoon, I would probably sign two more players, but I can't.'

Things looked good for a large part of the opening game at Derby and Leeds were 2-0 up after seventy-two minutes. Suddenly large holes began to appear in their defensive third and Derby eagerly exploited the opportunity. With Dean Sturridge in good form, the Rams poured forward and netted twice to level the scores. Lee Bowyer, who had a storming debut, restored

Leeds' lead with five minutes to go. Even then, the game was not dead and Derby managed to pull off another equaliser at the death.

A disappointing 2-0 defeat followed at home to Sheffield Wednesday, but scrappy single-goal victories against Wimbledon and Blackburn painted over the cracks. The points put Leeds in the enviable position of being able to go second if they could beat Manchester United at home. That was always going to be a big ask and the Red Devils ran out emphatic 4-0 victors. The sight of former cult hero Eric Cantona celebrating his goal and a masterly display in front of the Leeds fans was too galling for words. And it was certainly too much for Caspian, who promptly sacked Wilkinson. The decision looked premature but the manager had appeared to be on borrowed time from the minute that the sale of the club went through.

As inevitable as the inclusion of *Home Alone* in the Christmas television schedule, the appointment of former Arsenal supremo George Graham as the new manager of Leeds United was confirmed on 10 September, the announcement smacking of indecent haste. It came less than twenty-four hours after the press conference to confirm Wilkinson's sacking. He retained his composure and dignity throughout, but he was clearly devastated by the decision, distraught at not being allowed to complete the project he had begun eight years earlier.

'I'm very disappointed, very sad and obviously very shocked,' an emotional Wilkinson said at a hastily convened press conference. There was a group of fantastic young players coming through the youth development programme he had reinvigorated, but Wilkinson would not be the beneficiary. 'The whole place is much healthier, more vibrant, a potentially bigger place than anyone ever dreamt it could be eight years ago,' he sighed as he left. 'There aren't many clubs in a situation like ours who put up the vacant sign.'

Bill Fotherby claimed, 'It was the hardest decision of my life. It was like tearing a part of my body away, but I had lost confidence, and I was not going to let us get into the situation where we were in that gluepot down below and couldn't get out.'

Wilkinson's replacement surprised nobody. George Graham had long been touted as a possibility and soon became a certainty, seemingly the charismatic character that publicity-conscious owners coveted. Certainly, he was closely connected to Richard Thompson.

At a stroke, Graham was back at the top of the game after a year spent kicking his heels. He had been dismissed by Arsenal after being found guilty of taking a transfer bung.

The Scot was delighted by Caspian's faith in him. It looked something of an odd pairing, the smooth, naturalised Londoner and the club that epitomised dour Yorkshire grit, but it suited both Graham and Caspian. For him, it was a quick redemption, offering the chance to rub Arsenal's noses in it; for Caspian, it was a high-profile, go-ahead appointment that sat comfortably with their upwardly mobile ambitions.

The first game came quickly, with little time for Graham to change much in the background, but there was an instant success with Andy Couzens scoring in the first minute at Coventry. It was a false dawn. Coventry, managed by Gordon Strachan and including former Leeds men in McAllister and Noel Whelan, had something to prove. They quickly equalised and then Whelan came up trumps, scoring the decisive goal as City won 2-1.

McAllister, appointed as assistant to Strachan, was beaming after the game, offering some insight into goings on at Elland Road. 'The appointment of George Graham as manager was the best-known secret at Leeds, even before my transfer,' he said. 'As soon as the Caspian Group took over, he was linked with the job, so it came as no surprise to me when it happened. Howard spent money on the right sort of players, but then they got rid of him. It is strange he has been given the money, and then sacked so quickly.'

Graham was quickly given ample evidence of how big his task was. Two dreadful League Cup performances against Darlington and defeats to Newcastle and Leicester left Leeds in disarray, seventeenth in the table.

Two goals from the lively Rod Wallace snatched victory against Forest but then there were three straight defeats, including one by three goals at Arsenal. It was like a dagger through the heart of Graham, who had hoped to demonstrate to his former employees that he still had something to offer.

When Graham first met the Leeds players, he told them that they were in real danger of relegation and now he was acutely aware of the accuracy of his words. Pinning his plans on his core beliefs, he set about improving Leeds' defensive aspects. Loss of attacking threat was an acceptable consequence, he thought, but the Leeds followers despaired. Three victories in four games fooled no one and the three goalless draws that took the club into Christmas in a much healthier twelfth place heralded the dire football that was to follow – a team where the chief attribute was working hard was symbolised by Carlton Palmer and Ian Rush. The ungainly Palmer was restored to midfield, making Leeds' engine room an ugly place with little creativity; the once deadly Rush now toiled away on the right flank, frustrated by his teammates' inability to shoot on target. This was poor fare for the fans, but gates held up remarkably well, almost as if the supporters recognised they needed the purging parsimony of a drab year under Graham to get back on an even keel. Certainly, Graham's clarity of intention was a relief after the miserable inertia and vagueness of Wilkinson's final eight months.

The supporters accepted as inevitable Graham's priority of making Leeds difficult to beat, that most negative of ambitions. Lucas Radebe, reborn as a man-marking midfielder, typified what the manager wanted as he nullified opposing key men in game after game. This was grey football, even if it was effective.

The pick of the pre-Christmas results was the 2-0 defeat of Chelsea, with Rush getting his first goal for the club and Deane notching his second of the season on his fifth start.

Deane had been injured in the first game at Derby and Wilkinson had brought in on-loan Mark Hateley as cover, but he was a dismal failure. With Deane back and fully functioning, Leeds looked better, though they still struggled in front of goal.

Defeat at Coventry on Boxing Day was the first of three reverses in succession and reminded Graham that he could not afford to take things lightly. Leeds steadied with a seven-game unbeaten run, during which only two goals were conceded. All told, United kept twenty-three clean sheets in forty-five games, all but one with Martyn in goal. He was quite rightly elected the club's Player of the Year, proving time and again that he was the finest keeper in the country.

It was around this time that Graham made his first moves into the transfer market, his dealings eerily reminiscent of his later low-key moves at Arsenal. He recruited Norwegian utility defender Gunnar Halle and giant Dutch centre-back Robert Molenaar, quickly dubbed The Terminator for his uncompromising approach.

Lee Sharpe brought flair to midfield and scored some wonderful goals, which he celebrated in colourful fashion, notably an Elvis impersonation with the corner flag as a makeshift mic stand. However, he was an inconsistent presence, going missing for most of the winter.

Tony Yeboah was a shadow of the lethal and spectacular finisher he had once been, derided by Graham as unfit, overweight and out of form. He made only fleeting appearances under Graham and effectively secured his P45 when he petulantly discarded his shirt and hurled it at the bench after being subbed off at Tottenham in March. Graham took the gesture as a personal insult and in such circumstances there could be only one winner – the Ghanaian never got near a Leeds shirt again, departing for Hamburg SV a few months later.

Yeboah could have been the answer to Leeds' desperate need for goals, but the rift with Graham was too deep. The manager would contemplate no reconciliation, even when Leeds ended the season with a run of nine games which yielded four goals and not a single victory. A drab eleventh place was all a dour season merited.

CHAPTER TWENTY

Hasselbaink

George Graham refused to apologise for the negative approach in his first season – 'a necessary evil' was his summation. He promised a change of emphasis in the campaign that followed, telling the press that the quality of football would improve dramatically, with dour defensive ambitions ditched for a more entertaining approach.

> Having managed to save our Premier League status, this time I shall be looking for progression next season – with a top six place the target. With new players in the team then, hopefully, that will be a realistic target for us.
>
> I will be looking for us to be a lot more creative and to greatly improve our finishing and, more importantly, to play exciting football. I want to see people going forward and getting crosses in and shots on goal. I want to see goalmouth incidents and goals for the fans to go home afterwards saying, 'That was exciting stuff!'

Asked about his transfer plans, Graham said, 'When everyone seemed to be saying, "go out and panic buy," I refused. Teams have gone down after making rash signings and then they find themselves left with a player they may have paid £4 or £5 million for and put on an enormous salary. Hopefully, we will make good signings, players who will be proud to wear the Leeds United shirt. If there are any players who are not proud to wear it, they can go.'

Graham dismissed speculation that he had been targeted by Everton, telling the media, 'I am happy at Leeds, in fact I'm delighted to be Leeds United manager. As far as I am concerned, I'm going to be here to see the job though. I didn't come here for the short term. It's a big challenge, but one that I'm enjoying.'

Graham spent the summer reshaping his squad. Out went any of Wilkinson's men that he had decided were of no use to him. That included Tony Yeboah to Hamburg for £1 million, Brian Deane back to Sheffield United for £1.5 million, Tony Dorigo to Torino, John Pemberton to Crewe and Ian Rush to Newcastle. In September, Carlton Palmer followed, sold to Southampton for £1 million.

On the way in were two unknowns from Portugal's Primeira Liga: Vitoria Setubal midfielder Bruno Ribeiro and a Surinam-born striker going by the exotic name of Jimmy Floyd Hasselbaink, for whom cup finalists Boavista demanded £2 million. Graham also recruited three men in the mould of his more customary signings: Forest defender Alf-Inge Haaland (£1.6 million), Crystal Palace midfielder David Hopkin, who commanded the biggest fee at £3.25 million, and little-known Rangers left-back David Robertson.

There was also a shake-up behind the scenes, disagreement with Graham being the common theme as he lorded it over his new kingdom.

Director of youth coaching Paul Hart quit after a spat with Graham, complaining that he had no interest in the youth development programme, unwilling even to watch the youngsters.

The man who coached Leeds to Youth Cup triumphs in 1993 and 1997 left to take charge of Nottingham Forest's academy, saying, 'I've had five great years at Leeds but things have changed in the past year and the club is being run differently. I have explained my feelings to George Graham and I accept he has concentrated his energies on first-team matters since coming here. But I do find it astonishing that he has watched our youth team only three times since he took over as manager.

I fear the Caspian Group and the manager have no real insight into the ten-year plan laid down when Howard Wilkinson came in in 1988. We're just one year off seeing that plan come to fruition, but the long-term strategy is being ignored.'

Another man who clashed with Graham was Bill Fotherby. He took Graham to one side to push the cause of Yeboah, who he felt wasn't being given a fair chance. When Fotherby suggested that the Ghanaian should start against Chelsea, he was met with an icy glare. Graham sneered that Yeboah was unfit, overweight, and unready for action. Fotherby reminded Graham that he was the club chairman, only for Graham to superciliously remind him that 'in my contract with the club, it states I pick the team'.

A furious Fotherby took the matter to the board. But Graham was Caspian's man and they left Fotherby in no doubt that the manager enjoyed their unconditional support. From that day on, Fotherby was on borrowed time. His 'resignation' was confirmed on 25 September 1997, the club announcing that forty-five-year-old Peter Ridsdale would take over as club chairman.

'To become a director was a dream come true,' gushed a delighted Ridsdale. 'I never believed it would go beyond that, but I'm both honoured and proud to be chairman. Clearly, I have my own business to run, that takes up a large portion of my time, but I've been travelling to every home and away game over the last ten years, and spending time at Elland Road during the week. It will be a part-time capacity for me, as chairman, but I'm always on the end of the telephone.'

When asked about the matter, Fotherby revealed, 'They forced me out, I won't kid myself, they forced me out ... Caspian thought "young Ridsdale" was a genius, but I wouldn't let him run my errands. He killed everything we had built up with the help of the chairman, the board; he ruined it. I could see what they were doing, Ridsdale and his cronies.

God gave me a gift of convincing people that Leeds United was the best club in the world ... I would have stayed there until I died. It was my club. When I walked out of there, it broke my heart. It broke my heart and I've never been back.'

'Bill and I go back a long way, and I think he feels the time is right to go now,' lied Ridsdale, 'as there is somebody there capable of taking over from him.'

Leslie Silver remained a tokenistic member of the club board, but all the power had shifted to the plc. Despite being club chairman, Ridsdale had no vote where it mattered, though he would be the front man to represent United locally and nationally. 'I'll be part of the Caspian team, but obviously the figurehead.'

Graham had an ideal fixture to begin with, at home to former club Arsenal. Leeds fielded four of their summer signings including Hopkin, named by Graham as captain.

An end-to-end game was played in searing heat. Leeds started tamely before growing into the contest. They were rocked after thirty-five minutes when Ian Wright opened the scoring. United fought their way back and got the point they deserved when Hasselbaink levelled the score to send the crowd into raptures.

Midweek victory followed at Sheffield Wednesday but then United lost to Crystal Palace, Liverpool and Aston Villa without troubling the scorers.

The season came alive for Leeds on 14 September with a stunning 4-3 victory against high-fliers Blackburn at Ewood Park, all seven goals coming in a breathtaking first thirty-two minutes.

Leeds were sensational early on, punishing Rovers with two quick goals. Wallace turned in Kelly's downward header from 3 yards after three minutes, and then big Dutch defender Robert Molenaar volleyed in spectacularly from the edge of the penalty area.

Blackburn hit straight back; as the Leeds defence retreated in front of him, Kevin Gallagher chanced his luck, firing in from 25 yards.

Molenaar was harshly adjudged to have brought down Martin Dahlin after fifteen minutes, and Chris Sutton equalised from the spot.

The whirlwind start continued. Two minutes later after being found by Harry Kewell on the edge of the box, Rod Wallace beat four players before firing past a helpless Tim Flowers.

Penalty claims at both ends were rejected before Leeds restored their two-goal advantage when Hopkin slotted home low from 18 yards.

Blackburn made it 4-3 when Dahlin beat Molenaar and fired past Nigel Martyn.

Graham withdrew Molenaar at half-time – the Dutch defender had been given a torrid afternoon by Dahlin – and brought on Ribeiro, pulling Lucas Radebe back into defence. It brought order to the game, though Blackburn had the better of the second half.

Kewell received a second yellow card on seventy-eight minutes after interfering with a free kick and Leeds were forced into a rearguard action with Radebe marshalling his troops splendidly. They withstood frantic Rovers pressure to capture all three points and move into the top half.

Their upward momentum continued on 27 September, up to sixth after a superb victory over Manchester United.

Backed by a packed Elland Road, Leeds started brightly and dominated the opening half-hour. Gary Kelly's swinging free kick into the area caught the Reds defence out. David Wetherall threw himself at the ball as Gary Pallister and Peter Schmeichel dallied over which of them would take control. Before they could sort it out, Wetherall plunged in to power home a header, which sent the home fans wild.

While Leeds' start to the season had been promising, Hasselbaink's was less than auspicious. Graham had left him on the bench for the second game running after his indifferent form. Kewell's absence on international duty with Australia gave Hasselbaink the opportunity to restake his claim in the League Cup against Bristol City later that week.

He scored in the seventh minute but within half an hour he spoiled his night, sent off for retaliation against Brian Tinnion, meaning a three-match ban. Graham was furious, saying, 'I've no sympathy with him, if you raise your hands or arms then you deserve to go.'

Hasselbaink sat out games against Stoke, Newcastle (both of which were won handsomely) and Wimbledon. Defeat in the latter game saw Leeds slip back to eighth.

With Wallace doing the business, Graham was content to leave Hasselbaink on the bench even when he was available again. Wallace's eighth goal of the season was enough for Leeds to win at Tottenham. He was on target again in the following game, a clash with Derby that provided another goal fest.

A first victory at Elland Road since 1974 was in Derby's grasp after they took a three-goal lead inside thirty-four minutes, but they were denied by one of the most unlikely comebacks ever seen at the stadium.

The game was four minutes old when a poor defensive header from Robertson caught Martyn out. He could only drop the ball at the feet of Dean Sturridge, who lapped up the easiest of opportunities.

Graham's pre-match plans were left in tatters when another Martyn error gifted Sturridge a second on eleven minutes. The goalkeeper ran to the edge of his box to make a clearance, but Sturridge anticipated Martyn's movement and blocked the ball before steering a calm lob into the net.

Sturridge's second should have been Derby's cue to defend their unexpected lead, but the visitors continued to press forward and struck for a third time with little over half an hour gone. The unfortunate Robertson was penalised for a foul on Sturridge inside the box and Aljosa Asanovic made no mistake from the spot.

That should have wrapped up the result, but Leeds pulled themselves back into contention with two quick goals before the break.

Wallace started the fightback by turning Ribeiro's shot past Mart Poom on thirty-seven minutes and then a stunning left-foot volley from Kewell gave United the scent of victory. They could find no further joy, though, until Graham summoned Hasselbaink from the bench with thirteen minutes to go.

Almost immediately, he made it onto the scoresheet, converting from the spot after Christian Dailly was punished for handball. Half-time substitute Lee Bowyer completed a riotous recovery when he turned home Hasselbaink's pass with seconds remaining.

The topsy-turvy nature of the game was symptomatic of United's entire season, with Graham's customary defensive football cast to the four winds as Leeds yo-yoed around in the top eight. Successive goalless draws against Everton and Chelsea in December were aberrations. More typical was a 4-0 hiding handed out to Blackburn in March, followed by a five-goal victory at Derby. The goal rush owed much to Hasselbaink, who had caught fire after his slow start.

Two goals in a 3-1 victory against West Ham at the end of November evidenced the true quality of Hasselbaink's finishing and gave him the opportunity to showcase the cartwheel that would become his trademark celebration. A decisive second goal in the defeat of Bolton on 20 December began a spell of eight goals in ten appearances. He drew a blank in the next four games but then caught fire again with eight goals in eight matches.

The Bolton game coincided with the shock news that legendary United captain Billy Bremner had collapsed and died after a heart attack at the age of fifty-four. It was a tragically early departure of an outstanding servant to the club and a mood of despondency gripped the city. A minute's silence was held to commemorate the fallen warrior before kick-off of the following week's game at Chelsea. The match degenerated into a disgraceful kicking match, with Leeds' critics gleefully trotting out the 'Dirty Leeds' clichés.

Oliver Holt described it in *The Times* as 'like Mafeking or one of those great sieges that James Fenimore Cooper wrote about in *The Last of the Mohicans*. Fusillade after fusillade raked the Leeds United defences and prone forms, clutching at tired and injured limbs, littered their penalty area after every Chelsea attack. It was heroism after a fashion, an afternoon for anti-heroes, not heroes.'

Alfie Haaland and Gary Kelly paid the price before half-time, both men dismissed for some rough play. The incidents ruined the match as a contest with Leeds forced onto massed defence to preserve their clean sheet.

George Graham accepted the blame on behalf of his players, admitting that he was angered by some of their first-half indiscipline, but then accused some of the 'more technical' of the Chelsea players of overdoing things when they were tackled.

'In the second half,' Graham said, 'my players showed tremendous discipline. That helped the referee and he needed help. Players were going to ground very quickly, but I did not see the physio having to come on all that often. No one had to go off injured. We want the talented players and the skill, but let's leave the theatricals behind.'

It was in many ways a stereotypical Graham display, just like Arsenal in the old days, except this was 'Nil-nil to the U-ni-ted' rather than 'One-nil to the Ar-se-nal'.

If that was a triumph of sorts in the smoke, there was a near-disaster when Leeds returned to the capital, away to West Ham at the end of March. The game itself resulted in a spineless 3-0 surrender, but the real drama came as the Leeds party travelled back to Elland Road.

Players and officials cheated death when their flight back to Leeds-Bradford Airport crash-landed at Stansted Airport. As the plane accelerated down the runway, flames were spotted in the port side engine of the twin prop aircraft.

Passengers quickly alerted cabin staff and Captain John Hackett ordered the forty passengers and four cabin crew to brace themselves for an emergency landing. After a loud bang, the engine was engulfed in flames with the plane 150 feet above the runway. The captain had a difficult choice to make: he could bring the plane down or climb and hope the thinning oxygen would extinguish the blaze. Hackett opted to land an aircraft weighed down by 150 tons of fuel.

As it reached the runway, the plane careered off onto the grass, the nose wheel ripped away as the aircraft bounced its way to a messy halt.

As the passengers began to evacuate, the central exit door jammed and David O'Leary injured his shoulder as he barged it free. Others leapt from the rear of the plane and ran to safety as fire engines and ambulances screamed down the runway. Miraculously, there were no serious injuries.

After gathering in the departures lounge to make sure everyone was safe, club officials hired a fleet of buses to carry them safely home to Elland Road, where they arrived at 7.15 in the morning.

'We have had a hell of a result tonight,' said Peter Ridsdale. 'I was sitting in the centre of the plane, and just as the wheels started to leave the ground, I saw flames coming from the engine. A few seconds later there was a large explosion and the whole engine went up in flames.

At that stage we were still climbing. Almost immediately a buzzer went off and a stewardess said we were going to make an emergency landing and would we please be braced. We knew we were coming down. The flames were getting worse.

I could feel the heat on my right shoulder. You know the plane is full of fuel and you just hope you land before it explodes. The crew are heroes. The pilot subsequently told me he wouldn't have had time to go round again. He reckoned thirty seconds longer and the plane would have been up in flames.'

Gunner Halle praised the actions of O'Leary. 'David kept everyone's spirits up. I think everybody knew how serious it could have been. He was the first one to his feet and charged the exit so we could all get out safely. The flames were still burning fiercely when we climbed out. We all thought the plane was going to explode.'

The relief at a narrow escape was tempered by a splenetic spat with the local media. Following the FA Cup sixth-round defeat to Wolves, Stephen White, sports editor-in-chief of the *Yorkshire Evening Post*, wrote an open letter to Caspian chairman Chris Akers, criticising what he saw as a lack of investment.

'The statistics speak for themselves: the average price for top players in the Premier League is £5 million to £7 million. Leeds United have bought ten players at £11.5 million, average price £1.15 million. We are just not in the same bracket as the big boys. What is the priority of Leeds Sporting plc? Is it profit or success on the pitch?

You began by giving us one of the best managers in the game. Now let's get the players. As George himself says, "It would be lovely to be in a position where I could go out and buy players at £8 million and £7 million."'

Ridsdale retorted angrily, claiming that since its takeover of the club, Caspian had invested £16.1 million in new players in addition to paying off a debt of £2.8 million owed on Brolin and Yeboah. After deducting transfer receipts of £4.1 million, there had been a net spend of £14.8 million. This was in addition to the £16.5 million paid to acquire the share capital and the debt taken on of £11 million. The total investment stood at more than £42 million.

'For a club whose turnover is only 25 per cent of Manchester United's and half that of Liverpool and Newcastle, this represents substantial commitment and underlines our ambition,' insisted Ridsdale.

We are three points behind Chelsea and some 12 ahead of Tottenham. Neither of these clubs nor Leeds United's past track record suggest that high-priced stars are the solution to all problems. George Graham has underlined his desire to strengthen the existing squad as and when the right players become available. His teambuilding requirements have been supported to date and this support will continue. All of our fans should be reassured that our ambition matches theirs … We are committed to bring success once again to Leeds United. This will be built on solid foundations so that it is built to last.

If the manager comes to us, and says I want to sign X or Y, we will do everything in our power to deliver them for him. At the moment, we are not in a position where players have been identified, and we're saying you can't sign them. We have spent as much as anyone else since the takeover, but the problem we were faced with was the task was greater than with a lot of clubs. Other clubs are buying but they're also selling as well. George has bought nine players, but those players we've sold weren't worth a lot in the transfer market.

Managing director Jeremy Fenn was equally forthright:

Having secured the club's continued presence in the Premier League, [Graham] commenced a major squad rebuilding programme to put the team back into a position where it could once again challenge for major honours.

During the period under review, there has been a significant level of transfer activity … Since 30 June 1997, a further net investment of £2.9 million has been made to recruit David Hopkin and Alf Inge Haaland, whilst Tony Yeboah, Brian Deane, Ian Rush, Carlton Palmer, Tony Dorigo and Tomas Brolin have been sold.

It annoys me the way the press keep writing about us as though we don't spend money on players. It's simply not true. The accountants Deloitte and Touche showed in their recent report that in the last five years we are one of the top five net transfer spenders in English football. Their figures also show that over the last couple of years our net spend is almost £18 million which has only been bettered by Newcastle, Middlesbrough and Liverpool.

I think the major reason for the perception that we are low net spenders is simply because the manager has spent the money on a number of players to build up the squad rather than on a few high-priced, high-profile players.

The thin-skinned Ridsdale was badly stung by the criticism. He made a mental note for the future, determined that he would find a way to prove the doubters wrong.

Graham's shock reincarnation as the champion of attacking football was music to the ears of the board – the public lapped up the entertainment. When United won the title in 1992, the average league gate was 29,493. 1997/98 saw it soar to 34,641, the highest level since 1994 and the seventh highest in the Premier League.

Hasselbaink had an extraordinary season, finishing with twenty-two goals in forty games after taking what seemed to be an age to get going. It had the fans thinking that they had finally found a successor to Tony Yeboah. The Dutchman possessed neither the awesome shooting power of Yeboah nor his muscular build, but he was lithe and quick with an aptitude in front of goal that marked him out as one of the best strikers in England. Only Michael Owen, Dion Dublin and Chris Sutton scored more goals in the Premier League.

It looked like Caspian, George Graham and Leeds United were a dream ticket, with fifth place giving them a European place for the first time in three seasons. Everyone hoped that this time Leeds could make a genuine show of things in the UEFA Cup. Certainly, the striking partnership of Wallace and Hasselbaink and a vivacious supporting cast including mercurial Australian winger Harry Kewell had many people rating Leeds as a team that could shake up the top end of the table.

This looked nothing like a George Graham side, but who was complaining?

CHAPTER TWENTY-ONE

Goodbye, Gorgeous George

If anyone thought Leeds would build smoothly on George Graham's first full season in charge, they had not been around the club long enough. Just as the manager found a successful formula, Rod Wallace decided that seven years at Elland Road was quite enough, thank you, and declined the new contract on offer. He chose instead to head north to Rangers and signed a four-year deal with the Glasgow club. Wallace had formed a decent partnership with Jimmy Floyd Hasselbaink and the disruption was as welcome as a fart in a phonebox.

Graham went like for like by bringing in Dutch striker Clyde Wijnhard from Willem II for £1.6 million and spent the same amount on Chelsea's utility defender Danny Granville, but the supporters were distinctly unimpressed. They were even less amused when twenty-year-old Andy Gray decided he would have to look elsewhere to relaunch his career. Son of Frank and nephew of Eddie, Andy had come to prominence after being the one Leeds player to shine in the 1996 League Cup final but had been in Graham's starting line-up only once – his first game in charge.

'It's not been a surprise to me,' sighed Gray. 'I don't think my future will be at Elland Road, but it's difficult because all I ever wanted to do was to play for Leeds. I'd love to stay at Leeds and play football for the rest of my life, but at the same time, I need to go somewhere and play first-team football again, for the sake my own career.'

Gray moved to Nottingham Forest in a £200,000 deal, provoking unrest among supporters, but there was no shifting Graham on the matter.

He swatted away any criticism, supreme in his confidence that he knew what he was doing and was rewarded as his team began with a seven-game unbeaten run. On the downside, there were only two wins and there were widespread rumours that Graham's mind was on pastures new.

For the Scot, joining Leeds had always been more about himself, proving he could still do it and finding a way back into the big time, than any loyalty to Leeds. He cared little for the North, the club or the supporters, no matter what his public pronouncements. That much became patently clear to Peter Ridsdale when he met Graham to discuss the terms of his contract.

'Getting into Europe had nothing to do with me and everything to do with George Graham,' wrote Ridsdale in his autobiography. 'Whatever he was doing at Leeds, it was to demonstrate to his old club that they had been wrong to sack him ... George was more committed to success and proving his point than to proving his worth to Leeds United fans. But that hunger for success was something we could harness to our benefit.'

The pair sat down to discuss a new contract, with Ridsdale fully prepared to recognise Graham's achievement in getting Leeds back into Europe. What he wasn't prepared for, however, was the scale of Graham's demands; he asked for a £1 million salary and another million as his price for signing the deal.

'I almost spat coffee all over his lush carpet when he came out with his proposed package. He stared at me with the intent of a poker player who knew he had a royal flush. He knew, and I knew, that we couldn't afford to lose a manager who had just taken us into Europe. He also knew he was testing our ambition as a club. I was professionally paralysed in that instant, and said I'd take it to the board for consideration, knowing this would mean doubling his salary.'

The directors agreed to Graham's terms but insisted on the inclusion of a clause requiring any other club wanting the Scot to repay the signing-on money and pay up the remainder of his contract.

Graham wasn't overly impressed but had little choice other than to go along with the stipulation. It soon became a key issue. Tottenham chairman Alan Sugar approached Ridsdale with a request to speak to Graham and everyone knew what was going on when the manager quickly checked that Ridsdale would inform him if any club made a move for him.

In that instant, Ridsdale realised that Graham was not a man to be trusted and that he was patently aware of Sugar's interest. Ridsdale had told Tottenham that there was no way that Leeds would release Graham but Spurs' ambitions in that direction soon became the worst-kept secret in football – it was clear that Graham wanted the job and that Spurs wanted him.

Despite all the protestations of innocence and loyalty, the Leeds fans could read the writing on the wall and when Spurs hosted Leeds at White Hart Lane on 26 September, both sets of fans were heard chanting, 'F*** off Graham, F*** off Graham.' Spurs supporters would not easily embrace a man with such strong Arsenal connections and they made their feelings perfectly clear.

In advance of the game, Graham had said, 'I'm a professional, and I'm the manager of Leeds, we've got to go down there and get three points. It's 100 per cent wrong, we should be talking about football, the rest is just a side issue, nothing to do with the game. I'm going down there focused on getting three points and I'm sure the players will be well-focused as well.' His words prompted cynical sneers from the fans.

The game finished 3-3 with Spurs coming back from a 3-1 deficit and Graham chose to stay in London that evening rather than travel back to Leeds. Five days later, he was confirmed as the new manager of Tottenham, prompting Ridsdale to give chapter and verse on the matter in the matchday programme.

'George Graham's decision to leave Leeds United and become Tottenham's manager has saddened and disappointed me. We did all in our power to try and keep him, even to the extent of offering him a new role as football director ... That would have enabled George to spend a few more days a week in London, with a better balance between his working and personal life. I made the offer to George after our game at Tottenham last week, but it was not accepted.'

Ridsdale revealed that a year earlier he had responded to rumours about interest from Rangers and Tottenham by meeting Graham to discuss the situation. Capitalising on the gossip, Graham said that if Leeds could satisfy his financial demands he was prepared to sign a three-and-a-half-year contract and see it through.

A contract to that effect had been signed in December and Ridsdale was satisfied that Graham was at Elland Road for the long term.

'There is no doubt that, irrespective of winning trophies, and taking into account his signing-on fee, there would have been no manager in the Premier League to touch him financially. I would like to reassure everybody that the club went out of its way to remove any risk of people luring George away purely on a financial basis.'

Ridsdale used the opportunity to reiterate his claim that Leeds had always backed Graham in the transfer market. 'On no occasion has George Graham asked for cash for players that we have not provided. If I have a disappointment about our relationship it is only that, until the last couple of weeks, George has never gone on record as saying that we have committed the funds. In fact, there has been an implication that we have not supported him, and that is absolutely untrue.'

Ridsdale laboriously spelt out the details of Tottenham's badgering and the part played by Graham, revealing the depth of his annoyance. It all smacked of trying to curry favour with the fans, a 'Don't blame me' jibe. After a painstaking denunciation of the contribution of the press, he added. 'I might be chairman, but I am very much a fan, and I am going through what you are all going through. We are determined to build and not go backwards so it is our intention to obtain a top-quality manager who will take this club forward.'

Desperate to look good in the eyes of the fans, Ridsdale's exaggerated pleas revealed a trait that would come back to haunt him over the next few years.

He was determined to find the right man to replace Graham, someone who could take the project forward and on to the next level.

Putting the team under the temporary charge of Graham's assistants, David O'Leary and Eddie Gray, Ridsdale sounded out the dressing room about what he should do. He got laughed out of the place, derided as a naïve newbie – he'd made his bed, now he had to lie in it.

Ridsdale's democratic approach might have been the sort of thing that went down well in the corporate world, but in the more old-fashioned football industry it was taken as a lack of leadership. Ridsdale was forced to rely on his own instincts in seeking out a replacement for Graham.

The early betting quickly made former captain Gordon Strachan and Leicester's Martin O'Neill favourites to succeed Graham.

Seeing O'Neill up close when Leeds played Leicester on 3 October went a long way to convincing Ridsdale that the Foxes boss was the man for the job. Leicester looked good in securing victory, well-schooled by O'Neill. The Irishman seemed to have everything going for him – smart, articulate and, above all, young, all the things valued by the go-ahead plc that Leeds United had become.

Ridsdale was sold on the Irishman and O'Neill appeared to be likewise smitten, demanding that Leicester give him permission to speak to Leeds. For several days, the outcome seemed inevitable, but then O'Neill changed his mind, swayed by Leicester fans who begged him to stay. It was far removed from the way that Elland Road had implored Graham to 'f*** off' under similar circumstances.

The focus and betting switched to Strachan, but Ridsdale's thinking was once more shaped by the need to look good. The fans chanted O'Leary's name during a high-profile UEFA Cup-tie in Rome as Leeds played above themselves. They lost 1-0 but performed so admirably that Ridsdale turned to managing director Jeremy Fenn on the flight home and gushed, 'This man is going to be our next manager.'

At first O'Leary indicated he was not interested in the job as he weighed up an offer to follow Graham to White Hart Lane. 'It is an absolute pleasure to do the job in the short term,' he said 'though managing Leeds United is a big, big task and you need to be very experienced to take it on permanently. I've learned an awful lot from my time with George but being realistic I would like another couple of years of learning before managing a big club.'

A few days in charge swayed his views and he quickly made known his desire for the job.

'Now Martin is off the shortlist, we will have to look at other options,' Ridsdale told the press. 'David has always been on that list and with Martin now out of the running, he has clearly moved further up it.' He added that only three names originally made up that list – O'Neill, O'Leary and Strachan, who had long since fallen by the wayside.

'David has demonstrated in the way he has acted on a personal level and the way in which the team has responded in the last few weeks that it is only right he should be in our plans. I am delighted the fans have shown they are behind him. It's important that whoever we choose has their backing.'

O'Leary began to play hardball, peeved that he had not been the board's first choice. He did his best to screw promises of transfer money out of the directors.

'Coming off the plane [from Rome],' he commented, 'I was expecting Martin O'Neill to be here and that it would be a case of: "David, thanks very much and bye bye."

It's not my fault that the club has taken three weeks on the O'Neill issue. I do not believe that if it was anyone else coming into the job at Leeds, they would not want to find out about their contract or about the transfer budget before they signed. There is no reason why I should be any different.

I have not given the chairman a figure for transfers, but I would like to know what he has to offer. I still think we need to buy two or three players to be able to compete with the likes of Manchester United and Arsenal.'

Ridsdale was eager to allay O'Leary's fears, saying, 'We have made it clear that we will back whoever is manager here in the transfer market. We have outlined our plans to David and they are very similar to his own. He has not asked for a definitive amount of money and he would have been foolish to do so. He has talked to us about the players he admires and we have reassured him that we will do everything we can to attract them to Elland Road. In my opinion, the only reason he would turn this offer down now is if he thought he was not up to the job.'

It was a pointed challenge to O'Leary, paving the way for a defence if O'Leary rejected Ridsdale's offer.

The deal was done on the evening of Sunday 25 October, with O'Leary formally announced as the new manager via the club's website. He agreed a two-and-a-half-year deal carrying a near £700,000 salary, which would make him one of the highest-paid managers in British football.

'I was so certain of the outcome that I actually had the champagne on ice in the boardroom,' said Ridsdale. 'I am delighted that everything has now been sorted out and I am convinced that David will prove to be a very successful manager for Leeds United. He has already shown with his team decisions that he is going to be very much his own man. We have put his mind at rest about the question of money being made available for new players.'

The jury was out on a man with limited experience as the man at the controls, but he certainly talked a good fight and appeared to have the players fully behind him. George Graham had left the makings of a decent side in place but O'Leary would need to hit the ground running with Leeds at an important stage in an important season.

CHAPTER TWENTY-TWO

A Naïve Young Manager

As he took charge at Elland Road, David O'Leary made it known that he was his own man and had a clear vision for the club. That was the reason why, he said, he had been so careful in getting the commitment of the board to transfer funds before he accepted the job. He was as adept at public relations as his chairman, taking pains to emphasise his humility as he played down expectations.

'I'm just a naïve young manager' would become O'Leary's press conference catchphrase. It paved the way for him to claim overachievement in the months to come, but it was a double-edged sword, quickly becoming a cliché and a tool for his critics to use against him when the going got tough.

The manager enjoyed the normal early honeymoon period. Defeat at home to Leicester just before O'Leary became substantive saw Leeds drop to tenth, but a four-game unbeaten run in the Premier League propelled them up to sixth by 8 November. A League Cup defeat against Leicester was another reminder to Peter Ridsdale of the quality of Martin O'Neill, but that was rendered a minor footnote in Leeds' season by an extraordinary achievement at Anfield on 14 November.

Inspired by midfielder Jamie Redknapp, Liverpool bossed the first hour. The only thing missing was goals and after sixty-seven minutes the home side addressed the issue when Thompson's headed pass to the edge of the Leeds box brought Nigel Martyn rushing out. There was a fearsome clash with Liverpool striker Karl-Heinz Riedle with both men having eyes only for the ball. There was no intent, but an unforgiving referee awarded Liverpool a penalty. Robbie Fowler duly stroked home from the spot and it appeared that Leeds would suffer their customary hammering at Anfield.

With nothing to lose, O'Leary sent on eighteen-year-old striker Alan Smith for his debut. The change sparked a turning of the tide and was a crucial moment in the development of O'Leary's ethos.

Seconds after making his bow as a seventy-eighth-minute substitute for Clyde Wijnhard, Smith calmly slotted the ball home from 15 yards with his first touch of the ball in senior football. It looked as easy as a Sunday league game for the baby-faced striker who didn't have time to work out how to celebrate as his teammates mobbed him.

Almost immediately, a reinvigorated Hasselbaink added a second after breaking through a stretched Liverpool defence. Things got even better minutes later when a long ball found Hasselbaink out on the left. He cut inside, brushed past an opponent and fired into the far corner from the edge of the box.

O'Leary was in seventh heaven, his gamble on a callow teenager paying off handsomely. It typified the early weeks of his time in the job – eighteen-year-old Jonathan Woodgate, blooded a month earlier, was now a fixture at centre-back. O'Leary's selections were peppered with such precocious talent, with Ian Harte, Lee Bowyer (both twenty-one) and twenty-year-old Harry Kewell also featuring at Anfield.

These were the first fruits of a conveyor belt of talent, O'Leary reaping the benefits of Howard Wilkinson's grand plan. A succession of young gems had been nurtured by Eddie Gray and the departed Paul Hart – the latter could have been forgiven for a cheeky 'told you so' but just looked on approvingly from afar, satisfied he had the last laugh on George Graham.

'I'd been spotted by Leeds as a teenager, and from the moment I went there on trial I absolutely adored it,' recalled Woodgate. 'I loved the coaching, how the coaches spoke to the players, and the emphasis on developing the players as human beings as well as footballers. The coaches there were doing things with young players that were way ahead of their time … We had a hell of a youth team at Leeds. There was a ten-year plan for us to progress to the first team under Howard Wilkinson and George Graham. There was me, Harry Kewell, Stephen McPhail, Paul Robinson, Alan Smith and plenty of other quality players.

Then David O'Leary came in, and fair play to him for having some balls and giving so many of us youngsters a chance and letting us flourish. That was a great time. We were young, vibrant, exciting, fearless. And it was just like playing with your mates.'

Woodgate, in particular, benefited from O'Leary's tutelage, picking up all sorts of lessons from a man who had been one of the best centre-backs in the country for almost two decades.

Leeds followed up their success at Anfield with a 4-1 defeat of Charlton and though they lost at Old Trafford the following week, emphatic victories against West Ham and Coventry saw them move up to third.

The positive mood of Leeds supporters was further boosted by the return of local favourite David Batty, signed from Newcastle for £4.4 million. The thirty-year-old midfielder had left Elland Road for Blackburn six years earlier and was keen on a return 'home'. 'It has been an open secret that I wanted to come back to Leeds,' said Batty, while a beaming O'Leary added, 'I don't think he should have been allowed to leave the club in the first place.'

Batty might have been George Graham's final buy, but Newcastle dismissed a tentative enquiry in September. They rejected O'Leary's initial bid of £4 million, with manager Ruud Gullit harbouring hopes that Lucas Radebe might be included in any settlement. When it was clear that was not on, Gullit demanded £6 million. The difference in valuations was bridged when Batty's transfer request allowed Newcastle to avoid the payment of £800,000 in loyalty bonuses.

Batty's early weeks were unfortunate – he marked his debut against Coventry with a booking for a stereotypical sliding challenge on George Boateng. He set up one of Leeds' goals in a 2-0 victory but sustained a cracked rib that sidelined him for three months.

O'Leary's support for home-grown teenagers continued with Stephen McPhail's cameo appearances in midfield and goalkeeper Paul Robinson's constant presence on the bench. Both players were nineteen.

O'Leary claimed 'a special bond' with the players he now habitually referred to as 'my babies'. He lovingly recounted his own experience of playing in the Arsenal first team at seventeen. They trusted him, he said, and he would not 'allow anything to be done' that he felt 'was not right for them'.

In his own debut season as a player, O'Leary played the first forty league games before giving way to tiredness because 'I was creamed. I saw the same thing last year with Harry Kewell. Come March time, he was dead on his feet, just playing from memory.'

O'Leary's conviction regarding the quality of his youngsters grew even stronger as he watched them perform in three of United's biggest games of the season. Two UEFA Cup matches against the £50 million Roma team and a goalless draw against a star-studded Chelsea side were major proving grounds. 'Some wonderful experts were saying you can't compete with that many youngsters. The same people are now telling me what a great bunch of kids we have.'

O'Leary quietly sidelined Graham's more prosaic foreign signings, Robert Molenaar, Gunnar Halle and Marten Hiden. While some critics poked fun at O'Leary's cliché-laden interviews, United's football was infectious as they ripped into the best that the nation could offer with a fearless pressing game. Their verve was rewarded with unexpected popularity as Leeds reinvented themselves as everyone's 'favourite other team'.

They had a few dispiriting defeats along the way, but O'Leary's young guns gave some performances well beyond their years; a three goal victory at Newcastle on Boxing Day was the pick, though a 5-1 triumph at Portsmouth in the FA Cup pushed it hard.

When Pompey took the lead, the Fratton Park crowd sensed a shock, with memories flooding back of a 3-2 victory at Elland Road in the early days of George Graham's reign. Their hopes quickly crumbled – within eight minutes Leeds were in front, going on to win at a canter.

Missing eight players through injury and suspension, Leeds started with five defenders and finished with six players under twenty-three, including two teenage debutants in Matthew Jones and Tommy Knarvik.

Leeds went out in the next round at Tottenham but held up remarkably well in the league. Crowds flocked to see them – the 40,255 that witnessed the 1-1 draw against Manchester United on 25 April was the highest home league gate for five years. They were privileged to see Leeds give weight to the hopes of Ridsdale and O'Leary that they could be the team to end their opponents' domination of the English game, as Oliver Holt reported for *The Times*.

'Manchester United got a worrying glimpse of the future at Elland Road yesterday when a vibrant Leeds United side, buzzing with youthful energy and precocious skills, took them to the limits of their endurance … They also made a bold statement of intent. Ferguson has Arsenal and Chelsea to worry about this season, but this was a warning that next year, and in years to come, Leeds will be more concerned with emulating them than frustrating them.'

A week later Leeds cemented their place in the top four with a breathtaking 5-1 victory at West Ham. The Hammers were a threat to Leeds' top four aspirations but were put firmly in their place by a sublime performance. Hasselbaink's goal inside twenty seconds was a sign of things to come, and the dismissal of Ian Wright for two bookable offences after only eighteen minutes crippled West Ham's chances. Smith increased United's lead on the stroke of half-time and although Paolo Di Canio replied three minutes after the break, West Ham goalkeeper Shaka Hislop received the second red card of the game on the hour. Ian Harte converted the resultant penalty and Lee Bowyer and Alfie Haaland rounded off a crushing win. Still, the Hammers' misery was not yet complete – Steve Lomas was dismissed three minutes from the end.

Days later, Leeds lost by a single goal at Chelsea. Undeterred, they demonstrated that they genuinely had what it takes, delivering the Premier League title to Manchester United when they beat Arsenal with a Hasselbaink goal four minutes from the end of normal time.

With the clock running down, Kewell turned Lee Dixon inside out before crossing for Hasselbaink to head home. Leeds held on through six minutes of injury-time to secure a famous victory.

O'Leary and Ridsdale were delighted with the way the team flourished under the Irishman's leadership. Their team performances were uniformly impressive and the fourth place they secured was way beyond expectations. It represented a significant achievement at the end of a season which could have brought discontinuity following Graham's defection. O'Leary took to the job like he was born to it and his young squad oozed potential. The world waited to see how O'Leary's Babies would build on a campaign to remember.

CHAPTER TWENTY-THREE

A Meteoric Rise

The rise of Leeds United through 1999 was so meteoric that David O'Leary and Peter Ridsdale started to believe there was no limitation to what the club could achieve. They could see no reason why Leeds could not break the stranglehold that Manchester United had on English football.

Since Leeds themselves had been the last club to win the championship in the pre-Premier League era, only Blackburn in 1995 and Arsenal in 1998 had been able to break Old Trafford's title monopoly. At the end of the 1998/99 season, the Red Devils secured the treble of league, FA Cup and Champions League – no other side seemed to have it in them to end the Mancunian dominance, despite strong arguments from Liverpool, Chelsea and Arsenal.

'Why,' thought Ridsdale to himself, 'can't Leeds be the ones?'

The chairman was an unabashed admirer of Manchester United's commercial model and all his plans for developing Leeds as a business were lifted straight from the Old Trafford school of business enterprise. 'There was no reason in my mind why,' wrote Ridsdale in his autobiography, 'from performances on the pitch to season ticket sales to merchandise, we couldn't match Manchester United … David's persuasive argument that, if we invested in players, we'd reap rewards, started to bear fruit and we'd soon have Manchester United looking over their shoulders.'

There was one cloud on the horizon as the new season beckoned: the need to agree Jimmy Floyd Hasselbaink's new contract. It was a very big cloud.

Hasselbaink's rise since his arrival at Elland Road in 1997 was startling. The name meant nothing to anybody prior to George Graham's interest, but Hasselbaink had overcome a slow start to prove himself one of the best strikers around. Thirty-four goals in sixty-nine top-flight appearances for Leeds was clear evidence of that and his presence up front had become talismanic.

When it came to renegotiating his contract, the striker held all the aces, demanding a major improvement in terms to secure his continued loyalty to the cause. O'Leary desperately wanted to keep him, but not at any price, and discussions were difficult and protracted.

An improved four-year deal was offered, but didn't go far enough for Hasselbaink, who held out for a rise that would have blown the club's pay structure. The £30,000 per week salary he demanded would have been half as much again as any teammate, playing havoc with the admirable togetherness of the squad.

Each party ensured that the media received a clear briefing that the reason for the impasse was down to the other's intransigence and the war of words saw the relationship break down irretrievably. There was little surprise when Leeds accepted a club record fee of £12 million from Spanish club Atletico Madrid on the eve of the new season. Hasselbaink professed his love for Leeds and the supporters and insisted that he had never wanted to leave; Peter Ridsdale was equally adamant that the player had requested a transfer.

The money gave Ridsdale and O'Leary the wherewithal to refashion the squad and in came young Sunderland striker Michael Bridges for £4.5 million, while another £9 million went on strengthening the defence in the shape of Charlton's England Under-21 right-back Danny Mills and Chelsea centre-back Michael Duberry. O'Leary sprang a surprise with his fourth recruit, the obscure twenty-one-year-old Norwegian midfielder Eirik Bakke.

The signing of Bridges was fortuitous. The striker had all but agreed a £5 million move with Tottenham manager George Graham, but a meeting with abrasive Spurs chairman Alan Sugar gave Bridges second thoughts. Sunderland boss Peter Reid had already started spending the money, so a fallback deal was hastily set up with Peter Ridsdale, who delighted in undercutting Graham.

Leeds struggled to a goalless draw with Derby on the opening day of the season, prompting fears that the loss of Hasselbaink might prove fatal. Bridges' hat-trick at Southampton days later put an end to that debate.

By the time Leeds went to Old Trafford on 14 August, Leeds had further strengthened with the addition of Coventry speedster Darren Huckerby for another £5.5 million. He debuted in a three-man attack with Bridges and Harry Kewell, though Bridges was forced to limp out of the action after eighteen minutes. Leeds were playing well at the time and Kewell fired against the woodwork but two Dwight Yorke goals won the game for the home side.

Leeds bounced back with victory against Sunderland before stumbling at home to Liverpool. Their season was set up nicely, however, by uplifting wins at Spurs and Coventry and David O'Leary led an upbeat party into their first game in the UEFA Cup.

Their first-round opponents were Partizan Belgrade, with the away leg switched to Heerenveen in the Netherlands because of the conflict in Yugoslavia.

The change left United fans outnumbering their counterparts and they almost saw the perfect start with Gary Kelly shooting against the crossbar after seven minutes. Against the run of play, however, Partizan took the lead in the twentieth minute. When Nigel Martyn spilled Kezman's effort, Tomic was nicely placed to capitalise.

Happily, Lee Bowyer quickly equalised, volleying home left-footed from the edge of the area after keeper Damjanac flapped at a corner.

Things looked bleak when Lucas Radebe brought down Kezman in the area and there was little doubt about the penalty. Martyn saved Leeds' bacon and atoned for his previous error by saving Rasovic's spot kick. It swung the psychological advantage towards Leeds and Radebe gave them the lead with an overhead kick following a free kick.

They bossed the game thereafter and Bowyer sealed victory eight minutes from time, and progress was secured when Huckerby netted the only goal in the Elland Road return.

United were really up and running now – they enjoyed a wonderful spell, winning ten games in succession. Victory against Watford on 3 October saw them top the Premier League table for the first time since August 1995. They were also poised for the third round of the UEFA Cup after a 4-1 win at home to Locomotiv Moscow. Leeds were winning over the neutrals with their new brand of attacking football.

The winning sequence came to an end with a breathtaking 4-4 draw at Everton on 24 October. It was hell for leather excitement with Leeds coming from behind on three occasions before apparently securing the points when Woodgate nodded in their fourth goal. They were denied victory by David Weir's injury-time equaliser but won more friends with some high-tempo attacking play and spectacular goals. This was a team that played completely without fear, though O'Leary bemoaned their defensive naïvety.

Locomotiv presented no real barrier in the UEFA Cup and O'Leary's young guns turned on the style to dismantle the Russians en route to a 7-1 aggregate triumph. The manager continued to claim that Leeds were 'Babies' and he was just a 'naïve young manager', but he and everybody else knew that this was a very special side, one that was in with a real chance of capturing the league title.

The only threat to their momentum seemed to come with the inevitable dips experienced immediately after each Thursday night spent on UEFA Cup duty. A thirteen-game unbeaten sequence came to a sharp halt after the trip to Moscow, with Leeds losing 2-0 at Wimbledon on 7 November, losing top spot in the process.

They bounced back at the end of the month with a last-minute goal from Michael Bridges earning all three points at Southampton. The result saw them return to the top of the table.

They faced another Moscow team in the UEFA Cup. Spartak represented much stiffer opposition than Locomotiv, even though the first leg had to be played in Bulgaria because of the depth of the frost on Spartak's pitch.

Kewell headed against the woodwork early on and then opened the scoring after fourteen minutes, pouncing on a poor back pass before rounding the keeper and firing into an empty net.

Whether it was a readiness to settle for what they had or an improvement on Spartak's part, Leeds sat back and began to soak up the pressure, contenting themselves with the odd breakaway.

Nigel Martyn gave a tour de force performance but could do little when slack defensive play gave Shirko the room to control the ball before slotting home.

United's game plan had been based on Bridges' effectiveness at holding the ball up. That outlet was denied them when Bridges was laid low by injury and Spartak enjoyed all the pressure in the second half. They took the lead at the midway point when Brazilian striker Robson tapped home from 6 yards.

Spartak continued to press but Martyn and Co. somehow managed to shut them out. The narrowness of Spartak's advantage kept Leeds' interest in the trophy alive.

Lucas Radebe goals were like hen's teeth – few were as precious as his header with six minutes remaining in the second leg. It allowed Leeds to progress into the last eight by virtue of the away goals rule.

To boost their challenge, David O'Leary brought in Blackburn wide man Jason Wilcox in a £4 million deal. His arrival freed Harry Kewell up to operate as an out-and-out striker.

United's form in the Premier League was exceptional – two scores from Stephen McPhail saw Leeds shock Chelsea at Stamford Bridge in the week before Christmas.

Goals from Bowyer and Bridges in front of a 40,000 Elland Road crowd saw off Leicester on Boxing Day and cemented United's leadership of the Premier League table. The victory also extended an impressive run of results. In the twenty-three games played since losing to Liverpool in the final week of August, Leeds had lost just twice, and they and Manchester United were well clear at the top of the table with half of their fixtures played.

But, suddenly, the dark clouds of winter billowed in and Leeds United limped into the new millennium with a decidedly off-colour seven-day blip.

The Whites met fourth-placed Arsenal at Highbury on 28 December knowing that victory would extend their advantage over the Gunners to eleven points. That outcome never looked likely as Tony Adams and Co.

refused to be drawn into an irritable battle by the Leeds attackers who had so badly disrupted Chelsea a week earlier. In that game, Frank Leboeuf had been dismissed after petulantly stamping on Kewell as the winger turned him inside out. None of the Gunners' players lost their cool in that way.

Freddie Ljungberg and Thierry Henry scored the goals that brought Leeds' first defeat in seven matches.

Aston Villa's victory at Elland Road a few days later raised suspicions that Leeds might be about to implode. They put the doubters firmly in their place with an astonishing 5-2 victory at Manchester City in the FA Cup. Falling 2-1 behind within twelve minutes only seemed to whet Leeds' appetite.

This was Leeds at their free-flowing, irresistible best with Smith, Kewell and Bowyer cutting the hosts to ribbons. Kewell got two, Smith and Bowyer one apiece, with Bakke getting the other goal. It was the combination attacking movements which marked Leeds out as a class above, appearing likely to score every time they went forward.

They built on the success with victory at Sunderland, but then crashed out of the FA Cup at Villa. Leeds had been ahead but could do nothing as former Arsenal forward Paul Merson pulled all the strings for Villa and Benito Carbone played his finest game for the Midlanders, marking the occasion with a hat-trick.

Leeds continued to push hard in the title race, despite a 3-1 defeat at Liverpool. Manchester United opened their advantage to a telling six points, however, after a single-goal victory at Elland Road on 20 February.

Leeds should have got something out of the game but finishing was a differentiator – Andy Cole chipped over a backpedalling Nigel Martyn for the only goal and Leeds could not find a cutting edge when it mattered, denied by the woodwork on three occasions.

With ten minutes left, Bowyer fluffed a simple opportunity from 6 yards after Smith's shot came back off the post. On such moments are championships won and lost.

David O'Leary refused to concede the title, promising his young side would battle on. '[Manchester United] are the team that I've made favourites from day one but we're not going to give up hope ... We've got thirteen games left and we're going to try to win those thirteen games. We're a young emerging side learning our trade, playing against a great side and there wasn't much in the game ... I know what my side is about. We've had our little setbacks but we're a young side doing marvellously well.'

Leeds still had the UEFA Cup to keep them occupied; they were paired in the last eight with Roma, whom they had crossed swords with the previous year during O'Leary's first few weeks in the job.

The first leg in Italy showed exactly how far Leeds had come under O'Leary. They emerged with a goalless draw, despite being under constant pressure. Roma, inspired by Francesco Totti, penned them in for long periods and much of the credit for the result went to Nigel Martyn, unbeatable on the night.

'The defence was superb and it was an unbelievable achievement to come out of a game like that without conceding a goal,' said Peter Ridsdale. 'The country seems to think that Nigel Martyn is not the number one at the moment, but perhaps after that performance Kevin Keegan will disagree. The tie is set up nicely for next week.'

Leeds finished the job at Elland Road, though it was a tight affair with Roma showing their undoubted class.

After sixty-seven minutes, the irrepressible Kewell picked up the ball 25 yards out, beat a defender and rifled the ball home off the underside of the bar.

In the closing minutes O'Leary brought on Alan Smith for a tiring Michael Bridges and his aggressive play rattled the Italians. They lost their focus and momentum, preoccupied with sorting out Smith and two of their players were dismissed as Leeds ran down the clock.

O'Leary had a massive grin as he spoke to the press after the game, glorying in how far the team had come.

Slavia Prague came and went with a whimper in the quarter-finals – the 3-0 victory in the first leg at Elland Road made the tie a formality. Leeds were also boosted by decent victories in the Premier League against Coventry, Bradford and Wimbledon to maintain their pursuit of Manchester United. They were four points behind the Red Devils but had seven in hand on third-placed Liverpool.

Again, though, their spectacular progress hit some choppy water. With Turkish side Galatasaray awaiting in the last four of the UEFA Cup, Leeds' confidence was shaken by successive defeats, away to Leicester and at home to Chelsea.

O'Leary prayed that his men could get their act together as they prepared to face the Turks. Galatasaray fans were renowned for making visiting sides unwelcome. If anyone doubted the veracity of those accusations, Leeds' visit offered all the evidence that was needed. Two of the travelling supporters would never return to these shores.

Optimistic fans flew out intent on enjoying another marvellous evening. With an ironic poke at the expected 'Welcome to Hell' threat, they unfurled a 'Hello Hell, We are Leeds' banner as they left the plane at Istanbul airport the day before the game. O'Leary had expected 'a 100-strong rentamob', as he told the press, but the initial greeting from the locals allayed fears, with no hints of the horrors to come.

'I first went there for a friendly at the age of seventeen, so I knew what to expect,' said O'Leary. 'It's strange because, in general, Turkish people are lovely and look after you so well but when you fly in or get to the ground with a football team, you can't believe how hostile it is.'

As the evening wore on, all of that changed. Trouble started around 5 p.m. as a hundred or so Leeds fans congregated in local bars. Batu Dedeler, owner of the Riddim reggae bar, recalled: 'We did amazing business in one hour. They knocked back as much Elfe (lager), Jack Daniels and Bacardi as I could pour. Most were kind, but there were five or six really crazy guys. They carried beer glasses outside, we couldn't stop them, and others followed.'

Some of the Leeds fans began to engage in ugly banter with the locals. It didn't go down well but attending police did their best to keep a lid on the tension. After the inevitable scuffles broke out, the police moved fans on, but it displaced rather than ended the tension.

Rumours spread rapidly that Leeds fans were out for trouble and Galatasaray fans poured into town to check things out for themselves. With massed ranks of furious locals turning up, apprehension ran through the outnumbered Leeds supporters.

There is a difference of opinion regarding how the real trouble began, with Turks claiming that the visiting fans began hurling glasses – others reported that locals escalated matters by throwing chairs around. Whoever was to blame, things escalated quickly into a pitched battle.

A few hours later, Kevin Speight, forty, and thirty-seven-year-old Chris Loftus were dead from stab wounds. Loftus, a fibre optics engineer from Burmantofts, was in Istanbul with brothers Andy, Darren and Philip. He was stabbed through the heart as fighting broke out, and died shortly afterwards. Speight, a pub landlord from Farsley, died after three hours in intensive care, receiving treatment for a wound the length of his stomach. At least nine other people, including six Leeds fans, were injured.

'This was a premeditated attack,' said supporter Steve Wilkinson, who suffered knife wounds to one leg and a wound to his hand. 'We came out of a bar and there were 100 people waiting for us with machetes, knives, bits of chair and table legs and they just attacked us. The police did nothing; in fact they were helping them beat us up.'

Others suggested a group of Leeds supporters had attacked a lone Turk, possibly a taxi driver, who had then returned with a mob wielding knives and machetes.

Ridsdale's stock was never higher than during this tragic episode. He won plaudits for the calm and mature way he responded to the chaos. He remained in the hospital for hours, consoling friends and relatives.

The chairman had spent the evening dining with directors from Galatasaray when reports of trouble came through. He rushed to Taksim Hospital, near where the men were stabbed. As injured and angry Leeds fans were brought in, Ridsdale did what he could. When the hospital said they were short of blood supplies, he sent his chauffeur off to get more. He was with Darren Loftus, brother of Chris, when his body was identified.

Asked whether he thought the tie would go ahead the following day, Ridsdale said, 'It's too early to say. I am just trying to come to terms with the fact that I have seen a dead body for the first time in ten years. When you see a man having to identify the body of his brother with a massive stab wound in his chest it just isn't what you'd associate with football.'

Ridsdale did his best to persuade UEFA to postpone the game, but they refused. Galatasaray officials were immovable in their insistence that the fixture should go ahead and UEFA confirmed that if Leeds refused to play they would forfeit the game. The insensitivity of the Galatasaray officials extended to their refusal to countenance players wearing black armbands.

Ridsdale was appalled but helpless. After lengthy discussion, he sadly agreed to the game continuing despite all his misgivings. He felt he had no choice. 'The game has to be played at some stage and we accept that on balance under the circumstances it is a fair decision ... The reaction of the club is one of numbness and the reality will sink in when we get back, but clearly you don't expect when you set off to watch a football match to be dealing with such a tragedy. I would ask our supporters to understand that to do anything other than stay calm would be abhorrent. Football is not about travelling to watch a match and not returning home.'

The previous August, a life-size bronze statue of Billy Bremner had been erected in front of the club shop on the south-east corner of the Elland Road stadium. The monument became a focal point for supporters' tributes to their fallen comrades. Hundreds paid their respects by gathering at the stadium, leaving flowers, team shirts and scarves under the statue and tied to nearby railings.

A year later, a bronze plaque commemorating the incident and paying tribute to Chris Loftus and Kevin Speight was erected in a brick pillar in front of the shop just behind Bremner's statue.

Ridsdale hammered Galatasaray for their intimidatory tactics, both in the build-up to the match and during the game itself. He was appalled by the Turks' lack of regard for the loss of life.

Leeds players were subjected to death threats in their hotel rooms, and when they made their way from the coach to the stadium they ran the gauntlet despite protection from a cortege of riot police. After such a nightmare, drained players had little appetite for the evening's work.

'The right thing would have been not to have played it and if that meant forfeiting, that meant forfeiting,' said Nigel Martyn. 'The police had to jettison out of a load of trucks and jog alongside the coach as it went up to the stadium. It wasn't very pleasant. Myself and Paul Robinson went to warm up forty-five minutes before kick-off and there were policemen in the tunnel. They stopped us going out because they had to put their riot gear on. One group had their shields standing up against the ground and the others made like a roof at an angle for us to run out under.

There was all sorts getting thrown – coins, lighters, stones, everything you can think of. It was just wrong, really. The mood in the dressing room was different to how it was normally. You try and put it to the back of your mind and go out and perform and do the best you can, but there's no doubt it had an effect on us.'

The United supporters who made it into the Ali Sami Yen stadium showed what they thought of events, turning their backs to the pitch in protest as the teams lined up for the kick-off. In the circumstances, there could only be one outcome.

After twelve minutes, world-class midfielder Hagi found Arif out on the left and his pinpoint cross was headed in by Hakan Sukur from 6 yards, with the Leeds defence nowhere. The Turks doubled their advantage on the stroke of half-time, Oliviera Capone taking advantage of hesitation in the Leeds defence to force the ball home from 6 yards. The emphatic 2-0 victory was well merited.

UEFA decreed that Turkish fans should be excluded from the second leg and the game was played out in eerie surroundings at Elland Road. A banner proclaimed 'Welcome to civilisation', a barbed message for the benefit of the television cameras.

After a frantic start with Harry Kewell twice threatening the Galatasaray defence and Michael Bridges thwarted by Taffarel's legs, the Turks rocked United on six minutes. Leeds had already had a warning when Arif shot over after a mistake by Ian Harte. When Jonathan Woodgate brought down Sukur as he tried to round Martyn, Slovakian referee Lubos Michel pointed straight to the spot. Hagi's left foot did the rest despite Martyn guessing correctly. The goal left Leeds with a mountain to climb.

Back they came. Kewell went close as he forced Taffarel into another save. The Brazilian spilled the shot, but there was no Leeds player on hand to capitalise.

Sixteen minutes in, Leeds equalised. Jason Wilcox's corner was perfectly met by Erik Bakke, glancing his header in off the right-hand upright.

Hopes of a revival were undermined four minutes before the break when a quick Galatasaray break exposed Leeds' skeleton defence. Sukur rounded Mills and Woodgate before beating Martyn.

If that wasn't bad enough, Kewell was sensationally and unjustly sent off for supposedly stamping on Gheorghe Popescu. Television replays proved that no contact had been made, but the Romanian's play-acting conned the referee.

After sixty-eight minutes, Leeds equalised a second time. Galatasaray skipper Bulent nearly put through his own goal when he sliced an attempted clearance and from the resulting corner it was the old routine again, Bakke heading in from Wilcox's inswinger.

From somewhere, Leeds found their spirit. Bowyer had a shot blocked and Bakke went close to his hat-trick but just failed to get his head to another Wilcox corner. Wilcox himself had an opening following a run by Huckerby, but his shot was too close to Taffarel.

On a footballing front, the Turkish side had outclassed Leeds and were worthy winners. It was clear, though, that the shockwave of Istanbul had sapped the will of everyone connected with United. In such circumstances, no team could have hoped to perform at their best.

There was little appetite for playing football after such a tragic couple of weeks, but Leeds had to do what they could to get their season back on track. Their Premier League form had been disastrous with four straight defeats – a 4-0 hammering at home to Arsenal left the team in a limp fourth spot with five games to go. If they were to qualify for the Champions League, Leeds would have to find a way to overtake either Arsenal or Liverpool. They were level on points with the Gunners and five shy of the Merseysiders. Manchester United were streaking to the title with an eleven-point lead on Liverpool.

Arsenal's resolve strengthened over the home stretch – they already had a game in hand on their rivals and when they won four games on the bounce it took them clear in second. But the tide turned against Liverpool, who began to suffer with nerves as the finishing line neared.

On Friday 21 April, Liverpool were held to a goalless draw by Merseyside rivals Everton. Two days later, Leeds matched Liverpool, drawing 2-2 at Newcastle.

The following Saturday, Liverpool went down 2-0 at Chelsea. Leeds took advantage the next day with a spectacular 3-0 victory at Sheffield Wednesday, owing much to the in-form Harry Kewell. The Aussie wrapped things up with a lovely third, chipped from distance, as he celebrated his election as the PFA's Young Player of the Year.

Michael Bridges was also back on the goals trail – after a month without a goal, he broke his run at Newcastle and then scored again at Wednesday. When he added another in a 3-1 victory against Watford, Leeds were suddenly a point ahead of Liverpool, who inexplicably lost 2-0 at home to Leicester.

The following weekend, both sides were held at home. That left a one-game showdown with Leeds, away to West Ham, needing to match whatever result Liverpool could bring back from a trip to relegation-threatened Bradford City.

Liverpool were swept aside by a tide of emotion at Valley Parade. Former Leeds centre-back David Wetherall got the early power header that gave City the win they needed to keep them up. Gunnar Halle and Lee Sharpe were alongside Wetherall in the Bantams defence, having made the switch from Elland Road earlier in the season.

With Leeds playing out a sterile 0-0 draw at Upton Park, their dream was fulfilled – a place in the Champions League at the end of a testing season.

As the dust settled, David O'Leary reflected on a remarkable campaign:

> We've achieved my preseason target by finishing in the top three ... The last six weeks is best described as a ship that had brilliantly gone across the ocean three-quarters of the way, then the engines failed and we've limped into port. I thought we'd blown it, but Bradford have helped us out and good luck to them.
>
> When I took the job, people told me not to. They said the club was going nowhere but I think we've proven them wrong. I wanted to raise the profile of the club, make more people like us, get us playing attractive football and I think people now want to come here. I have to try and improve the quality of the squad but it's going to take time. We're not far away.

Asked about his own contribution, O'Leary played it down. 'I'm the young manager in the pack ... The experiences both on and off the field have had an effect and I'm now looking forward to a nice break.'

It was all for public consumption, however. O'Leary was brimming over with pride and satisfaction. He knew he had a remarkable team at his disposal and his confidence in his own abilities grew by the day.

CHAPTER TWENTY-FOUR

Reflections

The new millennium heralded a fresh and exciting era for Leeds United Football Club. David O'Leary's first full season in charge brought a coming of age for the club, the manager and the chairman. Securing a spot in the money-spinning Champions League was a game-changer, emphasising the team's potential as the 'Next Big Thing', genuine pretenders to Manchester United's crown. The way they set about the challenge won them admirers far beyond their local following.

Performances thrust O'Leary out of the shadow of George Graham as a great manager in his own right. The way his brash young men went about shaking up the best teams that Europe could offer was breathtaking, recalling Don Revie's golden age.

The Elland Road public loved it, with the average gate up by more than 3,000 to a shade under 40,000. Season ticket sales rose from 17,318 for 1997/98 to 23,400 for 1999/2000.

The club's financial health mirrored that of the football. A third successive year of profits bucked the historic trend – Leeds had previously only been kept afloat during years of penny-pinching by the largesse of Leslie Silver. Now it was a money-making machine: income from broadcasting fees of £22.6 million was almost triple that of 1998. The UEFA Cup run brought in almost £7 million, pushing turnover up to a record £57.1 million. In the last full year before the arrival of Caspian, turnover had been less than £15 million and the club had suffered a loss of £2.4 million.

The benefits of bringing in an experienced marketing man were evident. Bill Fotherby had done some fantastic commercial deals over the years but next to the smooth Adam Pearson he came across as a dodgy second-hand car salesman.

Merchandising income grew 35 per cent to £4.5 million, thanks to the launch of two new away kits and a month's worth of sales of the new Nike/

Strongbow home strip. Footfall at the redeveloped club shop at Elland Road was up and trading was brisk.

Pearson:

It is always so much easier to be successful commercially when the team is successful, and the team was about to embark on a very successful period. People in Leeds, and nationally and internationally, could see that. It was a very tight commercial team and one that worked extremely hard to secure some good, sound deals for the football club ... Packard Bell had been our sponsors at that time and we had just switched to Strongbow, which was a fantastic deal financially for the club ... Financially, we were talking top three or top four in the Premier League, which was great. Away from that, we put a whole cross-section of business partners together in a similar way to what they subsequently did at the Football Association. We had a level of six platinum sponsors below Strongbow who all contributed very significant funds to the sponsorship pot.

The deal with Nike was another game-changer, signalling a move into the big time. The entire atmosphere was different – forget the low-value local businesses that had been Fotherby's staple diet, Leeds had gone international and brought in the really big fish.

The Champions League promised even greater rewards with turnover about to go through the roof. £86 million! Leeds had never been anywhere near this status financially.

There was a reassuring safety net if the worst came to the worst – the board could recoup their investment by way of player sales. In 2001, sports finance expert Bill Gerrard placed a 'sell-on' value of £198 million on the squad, despite a book value of 'only' £64 million.

Howard Wilkinson might have been yesterday's man, but his ten-year plan was bearing wonderful fruit. Leeds had a side on the up, O'Leary's squad overloaded with exciting young footballers. They appeared ready to emerge as the team of the new millennium.

'I remember playing golf out in Girona with Johan Cruyff,' recalled O'Leary later. 'He told me we were like "football rock and roll". We are great to watch and we were a bit mad with it. We had a style of play that was completely different to the way others were playing at that time.'

There was a rumour in the summer of 2000 that AC Milan were preparing a £20 million bid for Harry Kewell while Juventus were said to be ready to offer £10 million for Jonathan Woodgate; O'Leary was forced to deny reports that he himself had been targeted by Celtic, saying, 'Who would want me? The only way I'll be leaving Leeds is if the chairman wants me to go and hopefully I'll be around for many years to come.'

Speculation was rife that Manchester United were eyeing O'Leary as successor to Alex Ferguson and the man himself revealed later that the Irishman would have been a strong runner if and when he decided to step down.

There was no disputing it – Leeds United was the club to watch.

Bring me my bow of burning gold;
Bring me my arrows of desire;
Bring me my spear: O clouds unfold;
Bring me my chariot of fire!

I will not cease from mental fight,
Nor shall my sword sleep in my hand:
Till we have built Jerusalem,
In England's green and pleasant land.

'Jerusalem' by William Blake

Bibliography

Bagchi, Rob, *The Biography of Leeds United: The Story of the Whites* (Vision Sports Publishing, 2020)

Batty, David, *David Batty: The Autobiography* (Headline Book Publishing, 2001)

Chapman, Daniel, *100 Years of Leeds United: 1919–2019* (Icon Books, 2019)

Chapman, Lee, *More Than a Match: A Player's Story* (Stanley Paul, 1992)

Gall, Caroline, *Service Crew: The Inside Story of Leeds United's Hooligan Gangs* (Milo Books Ltd, 2011)

Gray, Eddie, *Marching on Together: My Life at Leeds United* (Hodder & Stoughton, 2001)

Hodge, Steve, *The Man With Maradona's Shirt* (Orion, 2011)

Howe, Jon, *The Only Place for Us: An A–Z History of Elland Road – Home of Leeds United* (Pitch Publishing Ltd, 2015)

Jones, Vinnie, *Vinnie: The Autobiography: Confessions of a Bad Boy?* (Headline, 1999)

Ridsdale, Peter, *United We Fall: Boardroom Truths About the Beautiful Game* (Pan, 2008)

Saffer, David, *Sniffer: The Life and Times of Allan Clarke* (NPI Media Group, 2001)

Simpson, Dave, *The Last Champions: Leeds United and the Year that Football Changed Forever* (Bantam, 2013)

Sutcliffe, Richard, *Bremner: The Real King Billy* (Great Northern Books Ltd, 2011)

Thomas, Dave, *Jimmy Adamson: The Man Who Said No to England* (Pitch Publishing Ltd, 2013)

Wilkinson, Howard, and Walker, David, *Managing to Succeed: My Life in Football Management* (Mainstream Publishing, 1992)

Worrall, Frank, *Magnificent Sevens* (John Blake Publishing Ltd, 2007)